Praise for *Big Data Demystified*

"Big Data affects everyone. In this entertaining and thought-provoking book, Feinleib practically explains how, with the right tools in hand, Big Data can help you create a richer model of your organization and the wider world, recognize events you would not have discovered otherwise, and deliver a view of trends that can help you establish a competitive edge."

–Lars Björk,
CEO of QlikTech

"Dave's insight into the future of Big Data analytics and Operational Intelligence makes him one of the most relevant thought leaders in Silicon Valley."

–JoMei Chang,
CEO, Vitria Technology, Inc.

"Cutting through the hype and hubbub, David uncovers what matters most about Big Data: its business impact. *Big Data Demystified* is a road atlas for data-driven decision makers."

–Michael E. Driscoll,
CEO of Metamarkets

"Every business leader looking to create competitive advantage through data should stop and read this book. David shows us how to use Big Data to improve our organizations and our own lives."

–Roger Ehrenberg,
founder and managing Partner, IA Ventures

"*Big Data Demystified* is a must-read for anyone interested in Big Data. Feinleib doesn't just tell us which Big Data startups are poised to become tomorrow's breakout companies. He explains how we can use data to live healthier lives, improve our relationships, and better educate our children."

–Brad Feld,
managing director, Foundry Group

"Dave's book provides a useful tour of Big Data use cases, ranging from the sublime to the remarkable. The book takes on the concepts of how data collection, storage, and analytics are sparking a revolution in how we think about the world around us. It is an essential read for anyone who wants to expand their knowledge of what Big Data means for business, government, science, and ultimately for human kind."

–Sanjay Mehta,
vice president of product marketing, Splunk Inc.

"If you want to understand one of the most important trends to come along in decades, *Big Data Demystified* is for you."

–Cameron Myhrvold,
Ignition Partners

"*Big Data Demystified* is a comprehensive look at Big Data. David has taken a complex topic and simplified it for all of us."

–Ken Stephens,
senior vice president, Xerox Cloud Solutions

Big Data Demystified

How Big Data Is Changing The Way We Live, Love and Learn

by David Feinleib

Published by:

260 King Street, Suite 1309
San Francisco, California 94107

Visit our web site at
www.thebigdatagroup.com

ISBN-10: 061577461X
ISBN-13: 9780615774619

Library of Congress Control Number: 2013905570
The Big Data Group, LLC San Francisco, California

Printed in the United States of America

First Edition: May, 2013
10 9 8 7 6 5 4 3 2

Table of Contents

Introduction

If it's March or December, watch out. You may be headed for a break up. Authors David McCandless and Lee Byron, two experts on data visualization, analyzed ten thousand Facebook status updates and plotted them on a graph. They figured out that breakups spike around spring break and then again two weeks before the winter holidays.

If it's Christmas Day, on the other hand, you're in good shape. Fewer breakups happen on Christmas than on any other day of the year. If you're thinking that Big Data is an obscure topic with little relevance to your daily life, think again. Data is changing how dating sites organize user profiles, how marketers target you to get you to buy products, and even how we track our fitness goals so we can lose weight.

My own obsession with Big Data began while I was training for Ironman France. I started tracking every hill I climbed, mile I ran, and swim I completed in the icy cold waters of San Francisco's Aquatic Park. Then I uploaded all that information to the web so that I could review it, visualize it, and analyze it. I didn't know it at the time, but that was the start of a fascinating exploration into what is now known as Big Data.

Airlines and banks have used data for years to figure out what price to charge and whom to give loans to. Credit card companies use data to detect fraud. But it wasn't until relatively recently that data—Big Data, as it is talked about today—really became a part of our daily lives. That's because even though these companies worked with lots of data, that data was more or less invisible to us.

Then came Facebook and Google and the data game changed forever. You and I and every other user of those services generate a data trail that reflects our behavior. Every time we search for something, like someone, or even just visit a web page, we add to that trail. When Facebook had just a few users, storing all that data about what we were doing was no big deal. But existing technologies soon became unable to meet the needs of a trillion web searches and more than a billion friends.

These companies had to build new technologies for them to store and analyze data. The result was an explosion of innovation called Big Data. Other companies saw what Facebook and Google were doing and wanted to make use of data in the same way to figure out what we wanted to buy so they could sell us more of their products. Entrepreneurs wanted to use that data to offer better access to healthcare. Municipal governments wanted to use it to understand the residents of their cities better and determine what services to provide.

But a huge problem remained. Most companies have lots of data. But most employees are not data scientists. As a result, the conversation around Big Data remained far too technical to be accessible to a broad audience.

I had the opportunity to take a heavily technical subject—one that had a relatively geeky bent to it—and open it up to everyone, to explain the impact of data on our daily lives. This book is the result. It is the story of how data is changing the way we live, love, and learn.

As with any major undertaking, many people provided assistance and support, for which I am very grateful. I would like to acknowledge the companies I have worked with on market research and consulting engagements, including Aerospike, Cetas by VMWare, Cloudyn, Lattice, Lyris, New Relic, Newvem, Qliktech, and others. I would particularly like to thank Cameron Myhrvold for his mentorship and advice.

David Feinleib
San Francisco, California
May 2013

Chapter One

Why We Still Can't Predict Earthquakes

Although earthquakes have been happening for millions of years, and we have lots of data about them, we still can't accurately predict exactly when and where they'll happen. Thousands of people die every year as a result, and the costs of material damage from a single earthquake can run into the hundreds of billions of dollars.

The problem is that, based on the data we have, earthquakes and almost-earthquakes look roughly the same, right up until the moment when an almost-earthquake becomes the real thing. But by then, of course, it's too late.

And if scientists were to warn people every time they thought they recognized the data for what appeared to be an earthquake, there would be a lot of false-alarm evacuations. What's more, much like the boy who cried wolf, people would eventually tire of false alarms and decide not to evacuate, leaving them in danger when the real event happened.

Good Predictions Aren't Good Enough

To make a *good* prediction, therefore, a few things need to be true. We have to have enough data about the past to identify patterns. The events associated with those patterns have to happen consistently. And we have to be able to differentiate what looks like an event but isn't from an actual event. This is known as ruling out false positives.

But a good prediction alone isn't enough to be useful. For a prediction to be *useful*, we have to be able to act on a prediction early enough and fast enough for it to matter.

When a real earthquake is happening, the data very clearly indicates as much. The ground shakes, the earth moves, and, once the event is far enough along, the power goes out, explosions occur, poisonous gas escapes, and fires erupt. By that time, of course, it doesn't take a lot of computers or talented scientists to figure out that something bad is happening.

So to be useful, the data that represents the present needs to look like that of the past far enough in advance for us to act on it. If we can only make the match a few seconds before the actual earthquake, it doesn't matter. We need sufficient time to get the word out, mobilize help, and evacuate people.

What's more, we need to be able to perform the analysis of the data itself fast enough to matter. Suppose we had data that could tell us a day in advance that an earthquake was going to happen. If it takes us two days to analyze that data, the data and our resulting prediction wouldn't matter.

This, at its core, is both the challenge and opportunity of Big Data. Just having data isn't enough. We have to have relevant data early enough, and we have to be able to analyze it fast enough, that we have sufficient time to act on it. The sooner an event is going to happen, the faster we need to be able to make an accurate prediction. But at some point we hit the law of diminishing returns. Even if we can analyze in seconds the immense amounts of data required to predict an earthquake, such analysis doesn't matter if there's not enough time left to get people out of harm's way.

The Case Of The Italian Engineers

On October 22, 2012, six engineers were sentenced to six-year prison terms for inappropriately reassuring villagers about a possible upcoming earthquake. The earthquake occurred in 2009 in the town of L'Aquila, Italy and three hundred villagers died.

Could Big Data have helped the geologists make better predictions?

Every year, some 7,000 earthquakes of magnitude 4.0 or greater occur around the world. Earthquakes are measured either on the well-known Richter scale, which assigns a number to the energy contained in an earthquake, or the more recent moment magnitude scale (MMS), which measures an earthquake in terms of the amount of energy released.[1]

When it comes to predicting earthquakes, there are three key questions that must be answered: when, where, and how big?[2] In *The Charlatan Game*, Matthew A. Mabey of Brigham Young University argues that while there are precursors to earthquakes, "we can't yet use them to reliably or usefully predict earthquakes."

Instead, the best we can do is prepare for earthquakes, which happen a lot more often than people realize. Preparation means building bridges and buildings that are designed with earthquakes

---

1 http://www.gps.caltech.edu/uploads/File/People/kanamori/HKjgr79d.pdf
2 http://www.dnr.wa.gov/Publications/ger_washington_geology_2001_v28_no3.pdf

in mind and getting emergency kits together so that infrastructure and people are better prepared when a large earthquake strikes.

Earthquakes, as we all learned back in our grade school days, are caused by the rubbing together of tectonic plates—those pieces of the Earth that shift around from time to time.

Not only does such rubbing happen far below the Earth's sur-face, but the interactions of the plates are complex.[3] As a result, good earthquake data is hard to come by, and understanding what activity causes what earthquake results is virtually impossible.

Ultimately, accurately predicting earthquakes—answering the questions of when, where, and how big—will require much better data about the disparate natural elements that cause earthquakes to occur and their complex interactions.

Therein lies a critical lesson about Big Data: predictions are dif-ferent from forecasts. Scientists can *forecast* earthquakes but they cannot predict them. When will San Francisco experience another quake like that of 1906, which resulted in more than three thousand casualties? Scientists can't say for sure.

They can forecast the probability that a quake of a certain mag-nitude will happen in a certain region in a certain time period. They can say, for example, that there is an 80 percent likelihood that a magnitude 8.4 earthquake will happen in the San Francisco Bay Area in the next thirty years. But they cannot say with 100 percent certainty when and where that earthquake will happen, or how big it will be. This is the difference between a forecast and a prediction.[4]

---

3 http://www.planet-science.com/categories/over-11s/natural-world/2011/03/can-we-predict-earthquakes.aspx

4 http://ajw.asahi.com/article/globe/feature/earthquake/AJ201207220049

But if there is a silver lining in the ugly cloud that is earthquake forecasting, it is that while earthquake prediction is still a long way off, scientists are getting smarter about buying potential earthquake victims a few more seconds.

Unlike traditional earthquake sensors, which can cost $3,000 or more, basic earthquake detection can now be done using low-cost sensors that attach to standard computers, or even using the motion-sensing capabilities now built into many of today's mobile devices for navigation and game-playing.[5]

The Stanford University Quake-Catcher Network (QCN) comprises the computers of some two thousand volunteers who participate in the program's distributed earthquake detection network. In some cases, the network can provide up to ten seconds of early notification to those about to be affected by an earthquake. While that may not seem like a lot, it can mean the difference between being in a moving elevator or a stationary one, or being out in the open versus under a desk.

The QCN is a great example of the kinds of low-cost sensor networks that are generating vast quantities of data. In the past, capturing and storing such data would have been prohibitively expensive. But, as we will talk about in future chapters, recent technological advances have made the capture and storage of such data significantly cheaper—in some cases more than a hundred times cheaper than in the past.

Having access to both more and better data doesn't just present the possibility for computers to make smarter decisions; it lets humans become smarter too.

---

5 http://news.stanford.edu/news/2012/march/quake-catcher-warning-030612.html

5

How Data Makes Us Smarter

If you've ever wished you were smarter, you're not alone. The good news, according to recent studies, is that you can actually increase the size of your brain by adding more data.

To become licensed to drive, London cab drivers have to pass a test known somewhat ominously as "the Knowledge," demonstrating that they know the layout of downtown London's 25,000 streets as well as the location of some 20,000 landmarks.[6] This task frequently takes three to four years to complete, if applicants are able to complete it at all. So do these cab drivers actually get smarter over the course of learning the data that comprises the Knowledge?

It turns out that they do.

Data And The Brain

Scientists once thought that the human brain was a fixed size. But brains are "plastic" in nature and can change over time, according to a study by Professor Eleanor Maguire of the Wellcome Trust Centre for Neuroimaging at University College London.[7]

The study tracked the progress of seventy-nine cab drivers, only thirty-nine of whom ultimately passed the test. While drivers cited many reasons for not passing, such as a lack of time and money, certainly the difficulty of learning such an enormous body of information was one key factor. According to the City of London website,

---

6 http://www.tfl.gov.uk/businessandpartners/taxisandprivatehire/1412.aspx

7 http://www.scientificamerican.com/article.cfm?id=london-taxi-memory

there are just 25,000 licensed cab drivers in total,[8] or about one cab driver for every street.

After learning the city's streets for years, drivers evaluated in the study showed "increased gray matter" in an area of the brain called the posterior hippocampus. In other words, the drivers actually grew more cells in order to store the necessary data, making them smarter as a result.

Now, these improvements in memory did not come without a cost. It was harder for drivers with expanded hippocampi to absorb new routes and to form new associations for retaining visual information,[9] according to another study by Maguire.

In computers, advantages in one area also come at a cost to other areas. Storing a lot of data can mean that it takes longer to process that data. Storing less data may produce faster results, but those results may be less informed.

Take for example the case of a computer program trying to analyze historical sales data about merchandise sold at a store so it can make predictions about sales that may happen in the future.

If the program only had access to quarterly sales data, it would likely be able to process that data quickly, but the data might not be detailed enough to offer any real insights. Store managers might know that certain products are in higher demand during certain times of the year, but they wouldn't be able to make pricing or layout decisions that would impact hourly or daily sales.

---

8 http://www.tfl.gov.uk/corporate/modesoftransport/7311.aspx
9 http://www.ncbi.nlm.nih.gov/pubmed/19171158

Conversely, if the program tried to analyze historical sales data tracked on a minute by minute basis, it would have much more granular data, which could generate better insights, but such insights might take more time to produce. For example, due to the volume of data, the program might not be able to process all the data at once. Instead, it might have to analyze one chunk of it at a time.

The Power Of Efficiency

One of the amazing things about licensed London cab drivers is that they're able to store the entire map of London (within six miles of Charing Cross) in their memories, instead of having to refer to a physical map or use a GPS.

Looking at a map wouldn't be a problem for a London cab driver if the driver didn't have to keep his eye on the road and his hands on the steering wheel, and if he didn't also have to make navigation decisions quickly. In a slower world, a driver could perhaps plot out a route at the start of a journey, then stop and make adjustments along the way as necessary.

The problem is that in London's crowded streets no driver has the luxury to perform such slow calculations and recalculations. As a result, the driver has to store the whole map in memory. Computer systems that must deliver results based on processing large amounts of data do much the same thing: they store all the data in one storage system, sometimes all in memory, sometimes distributed across many different physical systems. We'll talk more about that and other approaches to analyzing data quickly in the chapters ahead.

Fortunately, if you want a bigger brain, memorizing the London city map isn't the only way to increase the size of your hippocampus.

The good news, according to another study, is that exercise can also make your brain bigger.[10]

As we age, our brains shrink, leading to memory impairment. According to the authors of the study, who did a trial with 120 older adults, exercise training increased the size of the hippocampal volume of these adults by 2 percent, which was associated with improved memory function. In other words, keeping sufficient blood flowing through our brains can help prevent us from getting dumber. So if you want to stay smart, work out.

Unlike humans, however, computers can't just go to the gym to increase the size of their memory. When it comes to computers and memory, there are three options: add more memory, swap data in and out of memory, or compress the data.

A lot of data is redundant. Just think of the last time you wrote a sentence or multiplied some large numbers together. Computers can save a lot of space by compressing repeated characters, words, or even entire phrases in much the same way that court reporters use shorthand so they don't have to type out every word.

Adding more memory is expensive, and typically the faster the memory, the more expensive it is. According to one source, Random Access Memory or RAM is 100,000 times faster than disk memory. But it is also about a hundred times more expensive.[11]

It's not just the memory itself that costs so much. More memory comes with other costs as well.

---

10 http://www.pnas.org/content/early/2011/01/25/1015950108.full.pdf
11 http://research.microsoft.com/pubs/68636/ms_tr_99_100_rules_of_thumb_
in_data_engineering.pdf

There are only so many memory chips that can fit in a typical computer, and each memory stick can only hold a certain number of chips. Power and cooling are issues too. More electronics require more electricity, and more electricity generates more heat. Heat needs to be dissipated or cooled, which in and of itself requires more electricity (and generates more heat). All of these factors together make the seemingly simple task of adding more memory a fairly complex one.

Alternatively, computers can just use the memory they have available and swap the needed information in and out. Instead of trying to look at all available data about car accidents or stock prices at once, for example, a computer could load yesterday's data, then replace that with data from the day before, and so on. The problem with such an approach is that if you're looking for patterns that span multiple days, weeks, or years, swapping all that data in and out takes a lot of time and makes it hard to find patterns.

In contrast to machines, human beings don't require a lot more energy to use more brainpower. The brain "continuously slurps up huge amounts of energy."[12] But all that energy is remarkably small compared to that required by computers.

"A typical adult human brain runs on around twelve watts—a fifth of the power required by a standard sixty watt light bulb." In contrast, "IBM's Watson, the supercomputer that defeated *Jeopardy!* champions, depends on ninety IBM Power 750 servers, each of which requires around one thousand watts." What's more, each server weighs about 120 pounds.

When it comes to Big Data, one challenge is to make computers smarter. But another challenge is to make them more efficient.

---

12 http://www.scientificamerican.com/article.cfm?id=thinking-hard-calories

Are Computers Smart?

On February 16, 2011, a computer created by IBM known as Watson beat two *Jeopardy!* champions to win $77,147. Actually, Watson took home a million dollars in prize money for winning the epic man versus machine battle. But was Watson really smart in the way that the other two contestants on the show were? Can Watson think for itself?

With an estimated $30 million in research and development investment, 200 million pages of stored content, and some 2,800 processor cores, there's no doubt that Watson is very good at answering *Jeopardy!* questions.

But it's difficult to argue that Watson is intelligent in the way that, say, HAL was in the movie *2001: A Space Odyssey*. And Watson isn't likely to express its dry humor like one of the show's other contestants, Ken Jennings, who wrote, "I for one welcome our new computer overlords," alongside his final *Jeopardy!* answer. What's more, Watson can't understand human speech. Rather, the computer is restricted to processing *Jeopardy!* answers in the form of written text.

The Problem of Speech

Why can't Watson understand speech? Watson's designers felt that creating a computer system that could come up with correct answers to *Jeopardy!* questions was hard enough. Introducing the problem of understanding human speech would have added an extra layer of complexity. And that layer is a very complex one indeed.

Although there have been significant advances in understanding human speech, the solution is nowhere near flawless. That's because, as Markus Forsberg at the Chalmers Institute of Technology points out, understanding human speech is no simple matter.[13]

Speech would seem to fit at least some of the requirements for Big Data. There's a lot of it, and by analyzing it, computers should be able to create patterns for recognizing it when they see it again. But computers face many challenges in trying to understand speech.

As Forsberg points out, we not only use the actual sound of speech to understand it, but also an immense amount of contextual knowledge. Although the words "two" and "too" sound alike, they have very different meanings. This is just the start of the complexity of understanding speech. Other issues are the variable speeds at which we speak, accents, background noise, and the continuous nature of speech—we don't pause between each word, so trying to convert individual words into text is an inefficient approach to the speech recognition problem.

Even trying to group words together can be difficult. Consider the following examples cited by Forsberg:

It's not easy to wreck a nice beach.
It's not easy to recognize speech.
It's not easy to wreck an ice beach.

Such sentences are very similar yet at the same time very different.

But computers are making gains, due to a combination of the power and speed of modern computers, combined with advanced

---

13 http://www.speech.kth.se/~rolf/gslt_papers/MarkusForsberg.pdf

new pattern recognition approaches.[14] The head of Microsoft's research and development organization stated that the company's most recent speech recognition technology is 30 percent more accurate than the previous version—meaning that instead of getting one out of every four or five words wrong, the software only gets one out of every seven or eight incorrect. Pattern recognition is also being used for tasks like machine-based translation, but as users of Google Translate will attest, these technologies still have a long way to go.

Likewise, computers are still far off from being able to create original works of content, although, somewhat amusingly, people have tried to get them to do so. In one recent experiment, a programmer created a series of virtual programs to simulate monkeys typing randomly on keyboards, with the goal of answering the classic question of whether monkeys could recreate the works of William Shakespeare.[15]

But computers are getting smarter. So smart, in fact, that they can now drive themselves.

How Cars Can Drive Themselves

If you've used the Internet, you've probably used Google Maps. The company, well known for its market-dominating search engine, has accumulated more than twenty petabytes of data for Google Maps.[16] To put that in perspective, it would take more than 82,000 MacBook Pro hard drives (at 256GB each) to store all that data.

---

14 http://www.nytimes.com/2012/11/24/science/scientists-see-advances-in-deep-learning-a-part-of-artificial-intelligence.html?pagewanted=2&_r=0

15 http://www.bbc.co.uk/news/technology-15060310

16 http://mashable.com/2012/08/22/google-maps-facts/

But does all that data really translate into cars that can drive themselves? In fact, it does. In an audacious project to build self-driving cars, Google combines a variety of mapping data with information from a real-time laser detection system, multiple radars, GPS, and other devices that allow the system to "see" traffic, traffic lights, and roads, according to Sebastian Thrun, a Stanford University professor who leads the project at Google.[17]

Self-driving cars not only hold the promise of making roads safer, but also of making them more efficient by better utilizing the vast amount of empty space between cars on the road. According to one source, some 43,000 people in the United States die each year from car accidents, and there are some five and a quarter of a million accidents per year in total.[18]

Google Cars can't think for themselves *per se*, but they can do a great job at pattern matching. By combining existing data from maps, with real-time data from a car's sensors, the cars can make driving decisions. For example, by matching against a database of what different traffic lights look like, self-driving cars can determine when to start and stop.

All of this would not be possible, of course, without three key elements that are a common theme of Big Data. First, the computer systems in the cars have access to an enormous amount of data. Second, the cars make use of sensors that take in all kinds of real-time information about the position of other cars, obstacles, traffic lights, and terrain. While these sensors are expensive today—the total cost of equipment for a self-driving equipped car is approxi-

---

17 http://spectrum.ieee.org/automaton/robotics/artificial-intelligence/how-google-self-driving-car-works

18 http://www.usacoverage.com/auto-insurance/how-many-driving-accidents-occur-each-year.html

mately $150,000—the sensors are expected to decrease in cost rapidly.

Finally, the cars are able to process all that data at a very high speed and make corresponding real-time decisions about what to do next as a result—all with a little computer equipment and a lot of software in the back seat.

To put that in perspective, consider that just a little over sixty years ago, the UNIVAC computer, known for successfully predicting the results of the Eisenhower presidential election, took up as much space as a single-car garage.[19]

How Computers Detect Fraud

All of this goes to show that computers are very good at performing high-speed pattern matching. That's a very useful ability, not just on the road but off the road as well. When it comes to detecting fraud, fast-pattern matching is critical.

We've all gotten that dreaded call from the fraud prevention department of our credit card company. The news is never good—the company believes our credit card information has been stolen, and that someone else is buying things at the local hardware store in our name. The only problem is that the "local" hardware store in question is five thousand miles away.

Computers that can process greater amounts of data at the same time can make better decisions, decisions that have an impact on our daily lives. Consider the last time you bought something with your credit card online, for example.

---

19 http://ed-thelen.org/comp-hist/UNIVAC-I.html

When you clicked that *Submit* button, the action of the website charging your card triggered a series of events. The proposed transaction was sent to computers running a complex set of algorithms used to determine whether you were you, or whether someone was trying to use your credit card fraudulently.

The trouble is that figuring out whether someone is a fraudster, or if you are who you claim to be, is a hard problem. With so many data breaches and so much personal information available online, it's often the case that fraudsters know almost as much about you as you do.

Computer systems detect whether you are who you say you are in a few basic ways. They verify information. When you call into your bank, and they ask for your name, address, and mother's maiden name, they compare the information you give them with the information they have on file. They may also look at the number you're calling from and see if it matches the number they have for you. If those pieces of information match, it's likely that you are who you say you are.

Computer systems also evaluate a set of data points about you to see if those seem to verify you are who you say you are, or at least reduce the likelihood of you being an imposter. The systems produce a confidence score based on the data points.

For example, if you live in Los Angeles and you're calling in from Los Angeles, that might increase the confidence score. However, if you reside in Los Angeles and are calling from Toronto, that might reduce the score.

More advanced scoring mechanisms (called algorithms) compare data about you to data about fraudsters. If a caller has a lot of data points in common with fraudsters, that might indicate that someone is a fraudster.

If the user of a website is connecting from a computer other than the one he's connected from in the past, he has an out-of-country location (say Russia, when he typically logs in from the US), and he's attempted a few different passwords, that could be indicative of a fraudster. The computer system compares all of these identifiers to common patterns of behavior for fraudsters and common patterns of behavior for you, the user, to see whether the identity confidence score should go up or down.

Lots of matches with fraudster patterns or differences from your usual behavior, and the score goes down. Lots of matches with your usual behavior and the score goes up.

The problem for a computer, however, is two-fold. First, it needs a lot of data to figure out what your usual behavior is and what the behavior of a fraudster is. Second, once the computer knows those things, it has to be able to compare your behavior to these patterns while also performing that task for millions of other customers at the same time.

So when it comes to data, computers can get smarter in two ways: their algorithms for detecting normal and abnormal behavior can improve; and the amount of data they can process simultaneously can increase.

What really puts both computers and cab drivers to the test, therefore, is the need to make decisions quickly. The London cab driver, like the self-driving car, has to know which way to turn and make second-by-second decisions depending on traffic and other conditions. Similarly, the fraud-detection program has to decide whether to approve or deny your transaction in a matter of seconds.

As Robin Gilthorpe, the CEO of Terracotta, a technology company, put it, "no one wants to be the source of a 'no,' especially when it comes to e-commerce." A denied transaction to a customer who is who she says she is, means not only a lost sale but an unhappy customer as well. And yet denying fraudulent transactions is the key to making non-fraudulent transactions work.

Peer-to-peer payments company PayPal found that out first-hand when the company had to build technology early on to combat fraudsters, as early PayPal analytics expert Mike Greenfield has pointed out.[20] Without such technology, the company would not have survived, and people wouldn't have been able to make purchases and send money to each other as easily as they were able to.

Better Decisions Through Big Data

When it comes to Big Data, we as human beings can still make bad decisions—such as running a red light, taking a wrong turn, or drawing a bad conclusion. But as we've seen in this chapter, we have the potential, through behavioral changes, to make ourselves smarter. We've also seen that technology can help us be more efficient and make fewer mistakes. The self-driving car, for example, can help us avoid driving through that red light or taking a wrong turn.

When it comes to making computers smarter, that is, enabling computers to make better decisions and predictions, what we've seen is that three main factors come into play: data, algorithms, and speed.

Without *enough* data, it's hard to recognize patterns. Enough data doesn't just mean having all the data. It means being able to run analysis on enough of that data at the same time to create algorithms that can detect patterns. It means being able to test the

---

20 http://numeratechoir.com/2012/05/

results of our analysis to see if our conclusions are correct. Sampling one day of data might be useless, but sampling ten years of data might produce results.

At the same time, all the data in the world doesn't mean anything if we can't process it fast enough. If you have to wait ten minutes while standing in the grocery line while a fraud-detection algorithm determines whether you can use your credit card, you're not likely to use that credit card for much longer. Similarly, if a self-driving car can only go at a snail's pace because it needs more time to figure out whether to move forward or stop, no one will adopt self-driving cars. So speed plays a critical factor as well.

We've also seen that computers are incredibly efficient at some tasks—analyzing vast quantities of similar transactions quickly such as trying to detect fraud. But they are still inefficient relative to human beings at other tasks, such as trying to convert the spoken word into text. That, as we'll explore in the chapters ahead, opens up one of the biggest opportunities in Big Data, an area called *unstructured data*.

Chapter Two

Big Data: What It Is and Why You Should Care

If there's one technology company that epitomizes Big Data, it's search engine giant Google Inc. According to industry research firm Comscore, Google handled some 12.2 billion search queries in March 2012.[1]

But Google doesn't just store links to the websites that appear in its search results. It also stores all the searches people make, giving the company incredible insight into the when, what, and how of human search behavior.

Those insights mean that Google can optimize the advertising it displays to monetize web traffic like almost no other company on the planet.

Not only can the company track human behavior, but it can also predict what people are going to do next. Put another way, Google knows what you're looking for before you do.

This ability to capture, store, and analyze vast amounts of human and machine data, and then to make predictions from it, is what's known as Big Data.

---

1   This chapter is an expanded version of an article published in *Harvard Business Review China*, January 2013.

Why 2012 Was The Crossover Year For Big Data

So why has Big Data become so hot all of a sudden? Why did *The New York Times* describe 2012 as the crossover year for Big Data?[2]

Big Data broke into the mainstream in 2012 due to a coming together of three trends.

First, multiple high-profile consumer companies ramped up their use of Big Data. Social networking behemoth Facebook uses Big Data to track user behavior across its network. The company makes new friend recommendations by figuring out whom else you know.

The more friends a user has, the more likely they are to stay engaged on Facebook. More friends means users share more photos, post more status updates, and play more games.

Business networking site LinkedIn uses Big Data to connect job seekers with job opportunities. With LinkedIn, headhunters no longer need to cold-call potential employees. They can find and contact them via a simple search. Similarly, job seekers can get a warm introduction to a potential hiring manager by connecting to others on the site.

LinkedIn CEO Jeff Weiner recently talked about the future of the site and its economic graph—a digital map of the global economy that will in real-time identify "the trends pointing to economic opportunities."[3] The challenge of delivering on such a graph and its predictive capabilities is a Big Data problem.

---

2 http://www.nytimes.com/2012/08/12/business/how-big-data-became-so-big-unboxed.html?_r=0

3 http://www.linkedin.com/today/post/article/20121210053039-22330283-the-future-of-linkedin-and-the-economic-graph

Second, both of these companies went public in 2012: Facebook on NASDAQ, LinkedIn on NYSE. Although these companies and Google are consumer companies on the surface, at the core, they are really massive Big Data companies.

The public offerings of these companies, combined with that of Splunk, a Big Data company that provides operational intelligence to mid- and large-size enterprises, increased Wall Street's interest in Big Data businesses.

As a result, venture capitalists in Silicon Valley are lining up to fund Big Data companies like never before. Big Data is defining the next major wave of startups that Silicon Valley is hoping to take to Wall Street over the next few years.

Accel Partners, an early investor in Facebook, announced a $100 million Big Data Fund dedicated to Big Data investments in late 2011 and made its first investment from the fund in early 2012. Well-known investors Andreessen Horowitz, Greylock Partners, and others have made a number of investments in the space as well.

Third, business users—active users of Amazon, Facebook, LinkedIn, and other consumer products with data at their core—started expecting the same kind of fast and easy access to Big Data at work that they were getting at home. If Internet-retailer Amazon could recommend books to read, movies to watch, and products to purchase, business users wondered why their own companies couldn't do the same thing.

Why couldn't a car rental company, for example, be smarter about which car to offer a renter? After all, the company has information about which car the person rented in the past and the current inventory of available cars. But with new technologies, the company also has access to public information about what's going on in a particular market, information about conferences, events, and other activities that might affect market demand, and availability.

By bringing together internal supply-chain data with external market data, the company should be able to more accurately predict what cars to make available, and when.

Similarly, retailers should be able to use a mix of internal and external data to set product prices and placement on a daily basis. By taking into account a variety of factors from product availability to consumer shopping habits, including what products tend to sell well with each other, retailers can increase average basket size and drive profits higher.

Google's Big Data Initiatives

Google's size and scale gives them access to a set of Big Data approaches most other companies simply don't have. One advantage Google has is an army of software engineers, which gives the company the ability to build Big Data technologies from the ground up. Google has also had to deal, for years, with massive quantities of unstructured data: web pages, images, and the like; rather than more traditional, structured data: tables that contain names and their associated addresses, for example.

Another advantage the company has is its infrastructure. The Google search engine itself is designed to work seamlessly across hundreds of thousands of servers. If more processing or storage is required or if a server goes down, Google's engineers simply add more servers. Some estimates put Google's total number of servers at greater than a million.

Google's software technologies were designed with this infrastructure in mind. Two technologies in particular, MapReduce and the Google File System, "reinvented the way Google built its search index," *Wired Magazine* reported during the summer of 2012.[4]

Numerous companies are now embracing Hadoop, an open-source derivative of MapReduce and the Google File System. Hadoop allows for distributed processing of large data sets across many computers.

While other companies are just starting to make use of Hadoop, Google has been using large-scale Big Data technologies for years, giving it an enormous leg up in the industry. In fact, just as others are adopting Hadoop, Google is shifting its focus to other, newer technologies. These include Caffeine for content indexing, Pregel for mapping relationships, and Dremel for querying very large quantities of data.[5]

Now Google is opening up some of that investment in data processing to third parties. The company introduced Google BigQuery, a web offering that allows interactive analysis of massive datasets, which means billions of rows of data, according to Google. BigQuery is data analytics on-demand, in the cloud.

Previously, companies had to buy expensive installed software and set up their own infrastructure to perform this kind of analysis. With offerings like BigQuery, these same companies can analyze large datasets without making a huge up-front investment.

---

4 http://www.wired.com/wiredenterprise/2012/08/googles-mind-blowing-big-data-tool-grows-open-source-twin/

5 http://www.wired.com/wiredenterprise/2012/08/googles-dremel-makes-big-data-look-small/

Google also has access to a very large volume of machine data generated by people doing searches on its site and across its network. Every time someone enters a search query, Google knows what that person is looking for. Every human action on the Internet leaves a trail, and Google is incredibly well positioned to capture and analyze that trail.

Yet Google has even more data available to it beyond search. Companies install products like Google Analytics to track visitors to their own websites, and Google gets access to that data too. Websites use Google AdSense to display ads from Google's network of advertisers on their own websites, so Google gets insight not only into how advertisements perform on its own site, but on other publishers' sites as well. Google also has vast amounts of mapping data from Google Maps and Google Earth.

Put all that data together and the result is a business that benefits not just from the best technology, but also from the best information. When it comes to Information Technology (IT), many companies invest heavily in the Technology part, but few invest as heavily and as successfully as Google does in the Information component.

Amazon's Impending Threat

Google isn't the only major technology company putting Big Data to work. Internet-retailer Amazon.com has made some aggressive moves and may pose the biggest threat to Google's data-driven dominance.

At least one analyst predicts that Amazon will exceed $100 billion in revenue by 2015, putting it on track to eclipse

Walmart as the world's largest retailer. Like Google, Amazon has vast amounts of data at its disposal, albeit with a much heavier e-commerce bent.

Every time a customer searches for a TV show to watch or a product to buy on the company's website, Amazon gets a little more insight about that customer. Based on searches and product-purchasing behavior, Amazon can figure out what products to recommend next.

And the company is even smarter than that. The company constantly tests new design approaches on its website to see which approach produces the highest conversion rate.

Think a piece of text on a web page on the Amazon site just happened to be placed there? Think again. Layout, font size, color, buttons, and other elements of the company's site design are all meticulously tested and retested to deliver the best results.

The data-driven approach doesn't stop there. According to more than one former employee, the company culture is a ruthlessly data-driven one. The data shows what's working and what isn't, and cases for new business investments must be supported by data.

This incessant focus on data has allowed Amazon to deliver lower prices and better service. Consumers often go directly to Amazon's website to search for goods or to make a purchase, skipping search engines like Google entirely.

The battle for control of the consumer reaches even further. Apple, Amazon, Google, and Microsoft, known collectively as the Big Four, are battling it out not just online but in the mobile domain as well.

With consumers spending more and more time on mobile phones and tablets instead of in front of their computers, the company whose mobile device is in the consumer's hand will have the greatest ability to sell to that consumer and gain the most insight about that consumer's behavior. The more information a company has about consumers in aggregate and as individuals, the more effectively it can target content, advertisements, and products.

Incredibly, Amazon's grip reaches all the way from the infrastructure supporting emerging technology companies, to the mobile devices on which people consume content. Years ago, Amazon foresaw the value in opening to others the server and storage infrastructure that is the backbone of its e-commerce platform.

Amazon Web Services (AWS), as the company's public cloud offering is known, provides scalable computing resources to emerging and established companies. While AWS is still relatively early, one analyst estimate puts the offering at greater than a $1.5 billion run rate per year.

Such computing availability is paving the way for new Big Data initiatives. Companies can and will still invest in building out their own private infrastructure in the form of private clouds, of course. But if they want to take advantage of additional or scalable computer resources quickly, they can simply fire up a bunch of server instances in Amazon's public cloud. This puts Amazon front and center not just with its own site and new mobile devices like the Kindle Fire, but with infrastructure that supports thousands of popular websites as well.

The result is that Big Data analytics no longer requires investing in fixed cost IT. Data capture and analysis can be done quickly and easily in the cloud.

Put another way, businesses now have the ability to capture and analyze an unprecedented amount of data—data they simply couldn't store before and had to throw away.

Realizing The Information Advantage

Infrastructure like Amazon Web Services, combined with the availability of open source technologies like Hadoop, means that companies are finally able to realize the benefits long promised by Information Technology (IT).

For decades, the focus in IT has been on the T—the technology. The job of the Chief Information Officer (CIO) was to buy and manage servers, storage, and networks.

Now, however, it is information and the ability to store, analyze, and predict based on that information that is delivering competitive advantage.

When IT first became widely available, those companies that adopted it early on were able to move faster and out-maneuver those that did not. Some credit Microsoft's rise in the 1990s not just to its ability to deliver the world's most widely used operating system, but also to the company's internal embrace of e-mail as the standard communication mechanism.

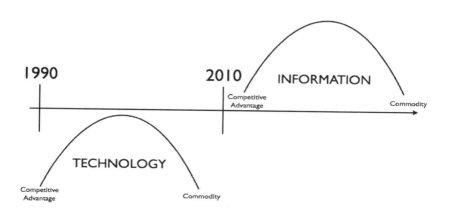

While many companies were still deciding whether or how to adopt e-mail, at Microsoft e-mail became the *de facto* communication mechanism for discussing new hires, product decisions, marketing strategy, and the like. While electronic group communication is now commonplace, at the time it gave the company a speed and collaboration advantage over those companies that had not yet embraced e-mail.

Companies that embrace data and democratize the use of that data across their organizations will benefit from a similar advantage. Companies like Google and Facebook have already benefited from this data democratization.

By opening up their internal data analytics platforms to analysts, managers, and executives throughout their organizations, Google, Facebook, and others have enabled everyone in the organization to ask business questions of the data and get the answers they need, and to do so quickly. As Ashish Thusoo, a former Big

Data leader at Facebook put it, new technologies have changed the conversation from "what data to store," to "what can we do with more data?"

Facebook, for example, runs its Big Data effort as an internal service. That means the service is designed not for engineers but for end users—line managers who need to run queries to figure out what's working and what isn't.

As a result, managers don't have to wait days or weeks to find out what site changes are most effective or which advertising approaches work best—they can use the internal Big Data service. And the service is designed with end-user needs in mind all the way from operational stability to social features that make the results of data analysis easy to share with fellow employees.

The past two decades were about the Technology of IT. In contrast, the next two decades will be about the Information of IT. Those companies that can process data faster and integrate public and internal sources of data will gain unique insights that will enable them to leapfrog their competitors.

As J. Andrew Rogers, founder and CTO of Big Data start-up Space Curve put it, "the faster you analyze your data, the greater its predictive value." Companies are moving away from batch processing (that is, storing data and then running slow analytics processing on the data after the fact) to real-time analytics to gain competitive advantage.

The good news for executives is that the information advantage that comes from Big Data is no longer exclusively available to companies like Google and Amazon. Open-source technologies like Hadoop are making it possible for many other companies, both established Fortune 1000 enterprises and emerging start-ups, to take advantage of Big Data to gain competitive advantage, and to do so at a reasonable cost.

The Big Data Disruption

The big disruption from Big Data is not just the ability to capture and analyze more data than in the past, but to do so at price-points that are an order of magnitude cheaper. As prices come down, consumption goes up.

This ironic twist is known as Jevons paradox, named for the economist who made this observation about the Industrial Revolution. As technological advances make storing and analyzing data more efficient, companies are doing a lot more analysis, not less. This, in a nutshell, is what's so disruptive about Big Data.

Many large technology companies, from Amazon to Google, and from IBM to Microsoft are getting in on Big Data. Yet dozens of start-ups are cropping up as well to deliver open-source and cloud-based Big Data solutions.

While the big companies are focused on horizontal Big Data solutions, smaller companies are focused on delivering applications for key verticals. Some products optimize sales efficiency while others provide recommendations for future marketing campaigns by correlating marketing performance across a number of different channels with actual product usage data.

The availability of these Big Data Applications, or BDAs, means that companies don't need to develop or deploy all Big Data technology in-house; in many cases they can take advantage of cloud-based services to address their analytics needs.

Big Data Applications

Big Data Applications represent the next big wave in the Big Data space. Industry analyst firm the 451 Group looked at the funding landscape for Big Data and reported that some $350 million had been invested in infrastructure-related Big Data plays as of November 2011. Since then, investors have continued to pour money into existing infrastructure players, putting another $65 million into Cloudera, a commercial provider of the Hadoop software, along with investments in other companies.

As a result, the focus is turning to the uses of Big Data instead of remaining on the infrastructure necessary to work with large amounts of data. Splunk, an operational intelligence company, is one existing example of this. Historically, companies had to analyze log files—the files generated by network equipment and servers that make up their IT systems—in a relatively manual process using scripts they developed themselves.

Not only did IT administrators have to maintain the servers, network equipment, and software for the infrastructure of a business, they also had to build their own tools in the form of scripts to determine the cause of issues arising from those systems. And those systems generate an immense amount of data; every time a user logs in or a file is accessed, every time a piece of software generates a warning or an error, that is another piece of data that administrators have to comb through to figure out what's going on.

With BDAs, companies no longer have to build the tools themselves. They can take advantage of pre-built applications and focus on running their businesses instead. Splunk's software, for example, makes it possible to find infrastructure issues easily by searching through IT log files and visualizing the locations and frequency of issues. Of course, the company's software is primarily installed software, that is, it has to be installed at a customer's site.

Cloud-based BDAs hold the promise of not requiring companies to install any hardware or software at all. In some ways, they can be thought of as the next logical step after Software as a Service (SaaS) offerings. SaaS products, that is, products delivered to customers over the Internet, are relatively well established. Salesforce.com, which first introduced the "no software" concept over a decade ago, has become the *de facto* standard for cloud-based Customer Relationship Management (CRM), software that helps companies manage their customer lists and relationships.

SaaS transformed software into something that could be used anytime, anywhere, with little maintenance on the part of the company itself. BDAs change the nature of those software companies by putting the focus on the data those software products store. Put another way, BDAs have the potential to turn technology companies into highly valuable information businesses.

In another example, oPower is changing how energy is consumed. The company tracks energy consumption across some fifty million US households by working with seventy-five different utility companies. The company uses data from smart meters—devices that track household energy usage—to provide consumers with detailed reports on energy consumption. Even a small change in energy consumption can have a big impact when spread across tens of millions of households.

Just as Google has access to incredible amounts of data about how consumers behave on the Internet, oPower has huge amounts of data about how people behave when it comes to energy usage. That kind of data will ultimately give oPower, and companies like it, highly differentiated insights. Although the company has started out by delivering energy reports, by continuing to build up its information assets, it will be well positioned as a Big Data business.[6]

BDAs aren't just appearing in the technology world, however. Outside of tech, companies are developing many other data applications that have an impact on our daily lives. In one example, some products track health-related metrics and make recommendations to improve human behavior. Such products hold the promise of reducing obesity, increasing quality of life and lowering healthcare costs.

The Move To Real Time

If the last few years of Big Data have been about capturing, storing, and analyzing data at lower cost, the next few years will be about speeding up the access to that data. If you've ever clicked on a website button only to be presented with a wait screen, you know just how frustrating it is to have to wait for a transaction to complete, or for a report to be generated.

Contrast that with the response time for a Google search result. Google Instant, which Google introduced in 2010, shows you search results as you type. By introducing the feature, Google ended up serving five to seven times more search result pages for typical searches.[7] When the interface was introduced, people weren't sure they liked it. Now, just a few years later, no one can imagine living without it.

---

6 http://www.forbes.com/sites/davefeinleib/2012/10/24/software-is-dead-long-live-big-data-2/

7 http://googleblog.blogspot.com/2010/09/google-instant-behind-scenes.html

Data analysts, managers, and executives want the Google Insight kind of immediacy in understanding their businesses. As these users of Big Data push for faster and faster results, just adopting Big Data technologies will no longer be sufficient. Sustained competitive advantage will come not from Big Data itself but from the ability to gain insight from information assets faster than others. Interfaces like Google Instant demonstrate just how powerful immediate access can be.

Your Big Data Roadmap

According to IBM, "every day we create 2.5 quintillion bytes of data—so much that 90 percent of the data in the world has been created in the last two years alone." Industry research firm Forrester estimates that the overall amount of corporate data is growing by 94 percent per year.

With this kind of growth, every company needs a Big Data roadmap. At a minimum, companies need to have a strategy for capturing data, from machine log files generated by in-house computer systems, to user interactions on websites, even if they don't decide what to do with that data until later.

As Rogers put it, "data has value far beyond what you originally anticipate—don't throw it away."

Companies also need to plan for exponential growth of their data. While the number of photos, instant messages, and e-mails is very large, the amount of data generated by networked "sensors" such as mobile phones, GPS, and other devices is much larger.

Ideally, companies should have a vision for enabling data analysis throughout the organization and for that analysis to be done in as close to real-time as possible. By looking at Google, Amazon, Facebook, and other tech leaders, companies can see what's possible with Big Data. What's needed is to put a Big Data strategy in place in your own organization.

Companies that have success with Big Data add one more key element to the mix: a Big Data owner. All the data in the world means nothing if you can't get insights from it. Organizations with a Big Data owner—a Chief Data Officer or a VP of Data Insights can help a company not only get the right strategy in place, but can also guide the organization in getting the insights it needs.

Companies like Google and Amazon have been using data to drive their decisions for years and have become wildly successful in the process. With Big Data, these same capabilities are now available to you.

Chapter Three

How Data Informs Design

How Data Informs Design at Facebook

If there's one company whose design decisions affect a lot of people—more than a billion of them—it's social networking giant Facebook. Quite often when Facebook makes design changes, users don't like them. In fact, they hate them.

When Facebook first rolled out its News Feed feature in 2006, back when the social networking site had just eight million users, hundreds of thousands of students protested.[1] Yet the News Feed went on to become one of the site's most popular features, the primary driver of traffic and engagement on the site, according to Facebook Director of Product, Adam Mosseri.[2]

That's one of the reasons that Facebook takes what Mosseri refers to as a data-informed approach, not a data-driven approach, to decision-making. As Mosseri points out, there are a lot of competing factors that can inform product design decisions. Mosseri highlights six such factors: quantitative data, qualitative data, strategic interests, user interests, network interests, and business interests.

---

1 http://www.time.com/time/nation/article/0,8599,1532225,00.html
2 http://uxweek.com/2010/videos/video-2010-adam-mosseri

Quantitative data is the kind of data that shows how people actually use the Facebook product, for example, the percentage of users who upload photos, or the percentage who upload multiple photos at a time, instead of just one.

According to Mosseri, 20 percent of Facebook's users—those who login more than twenty-five days per month—generate 85 percent of the site's content. So getting just a few more people to generate content on the site, such as uploading photos, is incredibly important.

Qualitative data is data like the results from eye-tracking studies. An eye-tracking study watches where your eyes go when you look at a web page. Eye-tracking studies give a product designer critical information about whether elements of a web page are discoverable and whether information is presented in a useful manner. Studies can present viewers with two or more different designs and see which design results in more information retention—important knowledge for designing digital books or building a news site, for example.[3]

Mosseri highlights Facebook's introduction of its Questions offering, the capability to pose a question to friends and get an answer, as an example of a strategic interest. Such interests might compete with or highly affect other interests. In the case of Questions, the input field necessary to ask a question would have a strong impact on the field, which asks users, "What's on your mind?"

Network interests consist of factors such as competition, as well as regulatory issues that privacy groups or the government raise. Facebook had to incorporate input from the European Union for its Places features, for example.

---

3 http://www.ojr.org/ojr/stories/070312ruel/

Finally, there are business interests—those elements that influence revenue generation and profitability. Revenue generation might compete with user growth and engagement. More ads on the site might produce more revenue in the short term, but at the price of reduced engagement in the long term.

One of the challenges with making exclusively data-driven decisions, Mosseri points out, is the risk of optimizing for a local maximum. He cites two such cases at Facebook: photos and applications.

Facebook's original photo uploader was a downloadable piece of software that users had to install in their web browser. On the Macintosh Safari browser, users got a scary warning that said, "An applet from Facebook is requesting access to your computer." On Internet Explorer, users had to download an ActiveX control, a piece of software that runs inside the browser. But to get the control installed they first had to find and interact with an eleven-pixel high yellow bar alerting them about the existence of the control.

The design team found that of the 1.2 million people whom Facebook asked to install the uploader, only 37 percent tried to do so. Some users already had the uploader installed, but many did not. So as much as Facebook tried to optimize the photo uploader experience, the design team really had to revisit the entire photo uploading process. They had to make the entire process a lot easier, not incrementally better, but significantly better. In this case, the data could help Facebook with incremental improvement, but it couldn't lead the team to a brand new design based on a completely new uploader.

With Facebook applications, such as well-known games like Mafia Wars and FrontierVille, the navigation framework that Facebook created on the site inherently limited the amount of traffic it could send to such applications. While the design team was able to make incremental improvements within the context of the existing layout, they couldn't make a meaningful impact.

As Mosseri puts it, "Real innovation invariably involves disruption." Such disruptions (like the News Feed) often involve a short-term dip in metrics, but they are the kinds of activities that produce meaningful long-term results. When it comes to design at Facebook, data informs design; it doesn't dictate it.

Mosseri highlights one other point about how Facebook has historically done design: "We've gotten away with a lot of designing for ourselves." If that sounds familiar, it's because it's the way that another famous technology company designs its products, too.

Apple Defines Design

If there is one company that epitomizes great design, it's Apple. As Steve Jobs once famously said, "We do not do market research."[4] Rather, said Jobs, "We figure out what we want. And I think we're pretty good at having the right discipline to think through whether a lot of other people are going to want it too."

When it comes to the world's most famous design company, a few things stand out, according to Michael Lopp, former senior engineering manager at Apple and John Gruber.[5]

First, Apple thinks good design is a present. Apple doesn't just focus on the design of the product itself, but on the design of the package the product comes in. "The build up of anticipation leading

---

4 http://money.cnn.com/galleries/2008/fortune/0803/gallery.jobsqna.fortune/3.html

5 http://www.pragmaticmarketing.com//resources/you-cant-innovate-like-apple?p=1

to the opening of the present that Apple offers is an important—if not the most important—aspect of the enjoyment people derive from Apple's products." For Apple, each product is a gift within a gift within a gift: from the package itself, to the look and feel of the iPad, iPhone, or Macbook, to the software that runs inside.

Next, "pixel-perfect mockups are critical." Apple designers mock up potential designs down to the very last pixel. This approach removes all ambiguity about what the product will actually look like. Apple designers even use real text rather than the usual Latin "lorem ipsum" text found in so many mockups.

Third, Apple designers typically make ten designs for any potential new feature. Apple design teams then narrow the ten designs down to three, and then down to one. This is known as the 10:3:1 design approach.

Fourth, Apple design teams have two different kinds of meetings each week. Brainstorm meetings allow for freethinking, with no constraints on what can be done or built. Production meetings focus on the reality of structure and schedule.

Apple does a few other things that set its design approach apart from others as well.

The company famously doesn't do market research.[6] Instead the company's people focus on building products that they themselves would like to use.

---

6 This myth has been dispelled, at least to some extent, by documents made public as a result of the Apple-Samsung court case, citing a recent market research study the company conducted: http://blogs.wsj.com/digits/2012/07/26/turns-out-apple-conducts-market-research-after-all/

The company relies on a very small team to design its products. Jonathan Ive, Apple's Senior Vice President of Industrial Design, relies on a team of no more than twenty people to design most of Apple's core products.

Apple owns both the hardware and software, making it possible to deliver a fully integrated, best of breed experience. What's more, the company focuses on delivering a very small number of products for a company its size. This is what allows the company to focus on delivering only best of breed products. Finally, the company has "a maniacal focus on perfection," and Jobs was said to dedicate half his week to the "high- and very low-level development efforts" required for specific products.

Apple is known for the simplicity, elegance, and ease of use of its products. The company focuses on design as much as it does on function. Jobs stated that great design isn't simply for aesthetic value—it's about function. The process of making products aesthetically pleasing comes from a fundamental desire to make them easy to use. As Jobs once said, "Design is not just what it looks and feels like. Design is how it works."

Game Design

Another area of tech in which Big Data plays a key role is in the design of games. Analytics allow game designers to evaluate new retention and monetization opportunities and to deliver more satisfying gaming experiences, even within existing games.[7] Game designers are able to look at metrics like how much it costs to acquire a player, retention rates, daily active users, monthly active users,

---

7 http://kaleidoscope.kontagent.com/2012/04/26/jogonuat-ceo-on-using-data-driven-game-design-to-acquire-high-value-players/

revenue per paying player, and session times—the amount of time that players spend each time they play.

Kontagent is one company that provides tools to gather such data. The company has worked with thousands of game studios to help them test and improve the games they create.

Game companies are creating games with completely customizable components. They use a content pipeline approach in which a game engine can import game elements, including graphical elements, levels, objects, and challenges for players to overcome.[8]

The pipeline approach means that game companies can separate different kinds of work: the work of software engineers from that of graphic artists and level designers, for example. It also makes it far easier to extend existing games by adding more levels, without requiring developers to rewrite an entire game.

Instead, designers and graphic artists can simply create scripts for new levels, add new challenges, and create new graphic and sound elements. It also means that not only can game designers themselves add new levels but players can potentially add new levels, or at least new graphical objects, as well.

Separating out the different components of game design also means that game designers can leverage a worldwide workforce. Graphic artists might be located in one place while software engineers are located in another.

Scott Schumaker of Outrage Games also suggests that a data-driven approach to game design can also reduce the risks typically associated with game creation. Not only are many games never completed, but

---

8 http://www.cis.cornell.edu/courses/cis3000/2011sp/lectures/12-DataDriven.pdf

many completed games are not financially successful.[9] As Schumaker points out, creating a great game isn't just about designing good graphics and levels; it's also about making a game fun and appealing.

It's difficult for game designers to assess these kinds of factors before they implement games, so being able to implement, test, and then tweak game design is critical. By separating out game data from the game engine it becomes far easier to adjust game play elements, such as the speed of ghosts in PacMan.

One company that has taken data-driven game design to a new level is Zynga. Well-known for games like CityVille and Mafia Wars, the social game maker is able to evaluate the impact of game changes nearly in real-time. Zynga's game makers can see how particular features affect how many gifts people send to each other and whether people are spreading a game virally or not.[10]

By analyzing data, Zynga was able to determine that in FrontierVille it was too hard for new players to complete one of their first tasks—building a cabin.[11] By making the task easier, a lot more players ended up sticking around to play the game. Although Zynga's public market value has fallen off significantly, there's clearly a lot to be learned from its approach to game design.

Better Cars With Big Data

What about outside the tech world? Ford's Big Data chief John Ginder believes the automotive company is sitting on immense

---

9 http://ai.eecs.umich.edu/soar/Classes/494/talks/Schumaker.pdf

10 http://www.gamesindustry.biz/articles/2012-08-06-zyngas-high-speed-data-driven-design-vs-console-development

11 http://www.1up.com/news/defense-zynga-metrics-driven-game-design

amounts of data that can "benefit consumers, the general public, and Ford itself."[12] As a result of Ford's financial crisis in the mid-2000s and the arrival of new CEO Alan Mulally, the company has become a lot more open to making decisions based on data, rather than intuition. The company is considering new approaches based on analytics and simulations.

Ford had analytics groups in its different functional areas, such as for risk analysis in the Ford Credit group, marketing analysis in the marketing group, and fundamental automotive research in the research and development department. Data played a big role in the company's turnaround, as data and analytics were called upon not just to solve tactical issues within individual groups, but also to be a critical asset in setting the company's go-forward strategy. At the same time, Mulally places a heavy emphasis on a culture of being data-driven; that top-down focus on measurement has had a huge impact on the company's use of data and its turnaround, according to Ginder.

Ford also opened a lab in Silicon Valley to help the company access tech innovation.[13] The company gets data from some four million vehicles that have in-car sensing capabilities. Engineers are able to analyze data about how people use their cars, the environments they're driving in, and vehicle response.

All of this data has the potential to help the company improve car handling, fuel economy, and vehicle emissions. The company has already used such data to improve car design by reducing interior noise, which was interfering with in-car voice recognition soft-

---

12 http://www.zdnet.com/fords-big-data-chief-sees-massive-possibilities-but-the-tools-need-work-7000000322/

13 http://blogs.wsj.com/cio/2012/06/20/ford-gets-smarter-about-marketing-and-design/

ware. Such data also helped Ford engineers determine the optimal position for the microphone used to hear voice commands.[14]

Big Data also helps car designers create better engines. Mazda used tools from MathWorks to develop its line of SKYACTIV engine technologies. Models allow Mazda engineers to "see more of what's going on inside the engine," and achieve better fuel efficiency and engine performance as a result.[15] Such models allow engine designers to test new engine components and designs before creating expensive prototypes.[16]

Historically, the challenge has been that internal combustion engines, which power most vehicles, have been incredibly hard to model. That's because they are inherently complex systems. They involve moving fluids, heat transfer, ignition, the formation of pollutants, and in diesel and fuel injection engines, spray dynamics.

Designers are also using data analytics to make decisions about how to improve race cars, decisions that could eventually influence the cars that consumers buy. In one example, the Penske Racing team kept losing races.[17] To figure out why, engineers outfitted the team's race cars with sensors that collected data on more than twenty different variables such as tire temperature and steering. Although the engineers ran analysis on the data for two years, they still couldn't figure out why drivers were losing races.

Data-analytics company Event Horizon took the same data but applied a different approach to understanding it. Instead of looking

---

14 http://blogs.wsj.com/cio/2012/04/25/ratings-upgrade-vindicates-fords-focus-on-tech/

15 http://www.sae.org/mags/sve/11523/

16 http://www.ornl.gov/info/ornlreview/v30n3-4/engine.htm

17 http://blogs.cio.com/business-intelligence/16657/novel-encounter-big-data

at the raw numbers, they used animated visualizations to represent changes in the race cars. By using these visualizations, they were quickly able to figure out that there was a lag time between when a driver turned the steering wheel, and when a car actually turned. This resulted in drivers making lots of small adjustments, all of which together added up to lost time. It's not enough just to have the right data. When it comes to design, as well as other aspects of Big Data, being able to see the data in the right way matters a lot.

Big Data And Music

Big Data isn't just helping us build better cars and airplanes. It's also helping us design better concert halls.[18] W.C. Sabine, a lecturer at Harvard University, founded the field of architectural acoustics around the turn of the twentieth century.[19]

In his initial research, Sabine compared the acoustics of the Fogg Lecture Hall, in which listeners found it difficult to hear, with the nearby Sanders Theater, which was considered to have great acoustics. In conjunction with his assistants, Sabine would move materials such as seat cushions from the Sanders Theater to the Fogg Lecture Hall to determine what impact such materials had on the hall's acoustics. Sabine and his assistants did this work at night, taking careful measurements, and then replacing all the materials by morning so as not to disturb the daytime use of the two halls.

After much study, Sabine defined the reverberation time, or "echo effect," which is the number of seconds required for a sound to drop sixty decibels from its starting level.[20] Sabine figured out

18 http://lib.tkk.fi/Dipl/2011/urn100513.pdf
19 http://en.wikipedia.org/wiki/Wallace_Clement_Sabine
20 http://www.aps.org/publications/apsnews/201101/physicshistory.cfm

that the best halls have reverberation times between two and two and a quarter seconds. Halls that have reverberation times that are too long are considered too "live," while halls with reverberation times that are too short are considered too "dry."

The reverberation time is calculated based on two factors: the room volume and the total absorption area, or the amount of absorption surface present. In the case of the Fogg Lecture Hall, where spoken words remained audible for about five and a half seconds—an additional twelve to fifteen words—Sabine was able to reduce the echo effect and improve the acoustics of the hall. Sabine later went on to help design Boston's Symphony Hall.

Since Sabine's time, the field has continued to evolve. Now data analysts are able to use models to evaluate sound issues with existing halls and to simulate the design of new ones. One innovation has been the introduction of halls that have reconfigurable geometry and materials, which can be adjusted to make a hall optimal for different uses, such as music or speech.

Ironically, classic music halls, such as those built in the late 1800s, have remarkably good acoustics, while many halls built more recently do not. This is due in large part to the desire to accommodate more seats, and the introduction of new building materials, which have enabled architects to design concert halls of nearly any shape and size, rather than being restricted by the strength and stiffness of timber.[21]

Architects are now trying to design newer halls to sound a lot like the halls of Boston and Vienna. Acoustic quality, hall capacity, and hall shape may not be mutually exclusive. By taking advantage of Big Data, architects may be able to deliver the sound quality of

---

21 http://www.angelfire.com/music2/davidbundler/acoustics.html

old, while using modern building materials and accommodating the seating requirements of today.

Big Data and Architecture

Concert halls aren't the only area of architecture in which designers are employing Big Data. Architects are applying data-driven design to architecture more generally. As Sam Miller of LMN, a one hundred-person architecture firm, points out, the old architectural design model was: design, document, build, and repeat. It took years to learn lessons, and an architect with twenty years of experience might only have seen a dozen such design cycles.

With data-driven approaches to architecture, architects have replaced this process with an iterative loop: model, simulate, analyze, synthesize, optimize, and repeat.[22] Much as engine designers can use models to simulate engine performance, architects can now use models to simulate the physical act of building.

According to Miller, his group can now run simulations on hundreds of designs in a matter of days, and they can figure out which factors have the biggest impact. "Intuition," says Miller, "plays a smaller role in the data-driven design process than it did in the analog process." What's more, the resulting buildings perform measurably better.

Architects don't bill for research and design hours, but Miller says that the use of a data-driven approach has made such time investments worthwhile, because it gives his firm a competitive advantage.

---

22 http://www.metropolismag.com/pov/20120410/advancing-a-data-driven-approach-to-architecture

Big Data is also helping design greener buildings by putting to work data collected about energy and water savings.[23] Architects, designers, and building managers can now evaluate benchmark data to determine how a particular building compares to other green buildings. The EPA's Portfolio Manager is one software tool that is enabling this approach. The Portfolio Manager is an interactive energy-management tool that allows owners, managers, and investors to track and assess energy and water usage across all of the buildings in a portfolio.[24]

Safaira offers web-based software that leverages deep physics expertise to provide design analysis, knowledge management, and decision support capabilities.[25] With the company's software, users can measure and optimize the energy, water, carbon, and financial benefits of different design strategies.

Data-Driven Design

In studying the design approaches of many different companies—and the ways in which data is used—what's clear is that data is being used more and more to inform design. But it is also clear that design, and the disruption that comes from making big changes, still relies on intuition—whether at Apple, Facebook, or elsewhere.

As Brent Dykes, evangelist of customer analytics at web-analytics company Adobe/Omniture, and author of the blog *AnalyticsHero,*

---

23 http://www.greenbiz.com/blog/2012/05/29/data-driven-results-qa-usgbcs-rick-fedrizzi

24 http://www.energystar.gov/index.cfm?c=evaluate_performance.bus_portfoliomanager

25 http://venturebeat.com/2012/04/10/data-driven-green-building-design-nets-sefaira-10-8-million/

notes, creativity and data are often seen as being at odds with each other.[26] Designers frequently view data as a barrier to creativity, rather than as an enabler of better design.

In one famous instance, Douglas Bowman, a designer at Google, left the company citing its oppressive, data-driven approach to design. Bowman described an instance in which a team at Google couldn't decide between two shades of blue, so they tested forty-one different shades between each blue to determine which one performed best.

Yet Bowman, now Creative Director at Twitter, didn't fault Google for its approach to design, which he describes as reducing "each decision to a simple logic problem,"[27] given the billions of dollars of value at stake. But he did describe data as "a crutch for every decision, paralyzing the company and preventing it from making any design decisions."

Dykes, in contrast, believes that the restrictions that data imposes increases creativity. Data can be incredibly helpful in determining whether a design change helps more people accomplish their tasks or results in higher conversions to paid customers on a website.

Data can help improve an existing design, but it can't, as Facebook designer Adam Mosseri points out, present designers with a completely new design. It can improve a website, but it can't yet create a whole new site from scratch, if that's what's required. Put another way, when it comes to design, data may be more helpful in reaching a local maximum rather than a global one.

---

26 http://www.analyticshero.com/2012/12/04/data-driven-design-dare-to-wield-the-sword-of-data-part-i/

27 http://stopdesign.com/archive/2009/03/20/goodbye-google.html

Data can also tell you when a design simply isn't working. As serial entrepreneur and Stanford University lecturer Steve Blank once said to an entrepreneur asking advice, "Look at the data." Blank was highlighting that the entrepreneur's thesis simply wasn't bearing out.

What's also clear across many different areas of design, from games to cars to buildings, is that the process of design itself is changing. The cycle of creating a design and testing it out is becoming a lot shorter due to the use of Big Data resources.

The process of getting data on an existing design and figuring out what's wrong or how to incrementally improve it is also happening much faster, both online and offline. Low-cost data collection and computer resources are playing a big role in speeding up the process of design, testing, and redesign. That, in turn, is enabling people to have not only their designs, but the design processes themselves, informed by design.

Website Design

As compelling as all that is, however, many of us will never get to design a smartphone, a car, or a building. But creating a website is something nearly anyone can do. And millions of people do.

As of December 2011, there were 555 million websites, 300 million of which were added during that year.[28] Websites aren't just the purview of big companies. Small business owners and individuals have built more than twenty-six million websites using a free website-design tool called Wix.

---

28 http://royal.pingdom.com/2012/01/17/internet-2011-in-numbers/

While web analytics—the tools used to track site visits, to test which version of a web page works better, and to measure conversions of visitors to customers—has come a long way in the last decade, in terms of becoming data-driven, web design itself has not progressed much in the same period of time, says Dykes.

Ironically, web design is one of the easiest forms of design to measure. Every page, button, and graphic can be instrumented, and designers and marketers can evaluate not just on-site design but the impact of advertising, other sites a user has visited, and numerous other off-site factors as well.

There are lots of web-analytics tools available, but many of these tools require heavy analytics expertise or are primarily targeted at technologists, not marketers. Solutions like Adobe Test&Target (formerly Omniture Test&Target) and Google Analytics Content Experiments provide the ability to test out different designs, but still require technical expertise. More recently introduced offerings, such as Optimizely, hold the promise of making the creation and running of site-optimization tests easier.

What's more, at large companies, making changes to a company's website remains a time-consuming and difficult process, one that involves working with relatively inflexible content-management systems and quite often, IT departments that already have too much work to do. Thus, while experimenting with new designs, graphics, layouts, and the like should be easy, it's still quite difficult. A web-site overhaul is usually a major project, not a simple change.

Many content-management systems rely on a single template for an entire site, and while they make it easy to add, edit, or remove individual pages, create a blog post, or add a whitepaper, changing the actual site design is hard. Typically there's no integrated, easy way to tweak a layout or test different designs. Such changes require the involvement of a web developer.

Such systems frequently lack built-in staging capabilities. A major change is either live, or it isn't. And unlike systems like Facebook, which can roll out changes to a subset of users and get feedback on them, many content management systems have no such capability. Facebook can roll out changes to a subset of users on a very finely targeted basis: to a specific percentage of its user base, males or females only, people with or without certain affiliations, members of certain groups, or based on other characteristics.

This makes changes and new features relatively low risk. In contrast, major changes to most corporate websites are relatively high-risk due to the inability to roll out changes to a subset of a site's visitors. What's more, most content management systems use pages and posts as the fundamental building block of design. The other design elements are typically static. In contrast, a site like Facebook may have many modules that make up a particular page or the site as a whole, making any individual module easier to change.

Marketing execs are often concerned about losing inbound links that reference a particular piece of content. As a result, marketing executives and IT managers alike are loath to make and test such changes on a frequent basis.

There are lots of tools available to help marketers understand how to design their sites for better conversion. The lack of data-driven design when it comes to websites, however, may have more to do with the limitations of underlying content management systems and the restrictions they impose than with the point tools available to inform marketers about what they need to fix.

Yet website designers and marketers recognize that they need to change. Static websites no longer garner as much traffic in Google. Fresh, current websites that act a lot more like news sites get indexed better in Google and are more likely to have content shared on social media like Twitter, Facebook, LinkedIn, blogs, and news sites.

Newer sites—and modern marketing departments—are a lot more focused on creating and delivering content that appeals to actual prospects, rather than to Google's website crawlers. In large part, this is due to Google's recent algorithm changes, which have placed more emphasis on useful, current, and authoritative content.

Going forward, it will no longer be enough to have a poor landing page for a customer to land on. Websites will need to be visually appealing, informative, and specifically designed to draw prospects in and convert them into customers.

As social media and search change to become more focused on content that's interesting and relevant to human beings, marketers and website designers will need to change too. They'll need to place more emphasis on data-driven design to create websites and content that appeals to human beings—not machines. Both on and off the web, we will need to create designs and implement design approaches informed by data. Of course, the design tools we use will need to change as well.

Chapter Four

Why A Picture Is Worth A Thousand Words

It's your first ever visit to Washington, DC. Arriving in the capital of the United States, you're excited to visit all the monuments and museums, the White House, and the Washington Monument. To get from one place to another you need to take the local public transit system, the Metro. That seems easy enough. There's just one problem: you don't have a map.[1]

Instead of a map, imagine that the nice gentleman in the information booth hands you an alphabetized list of stations, line names, and coordinates. In theory, you have all the information you need to navigate the DC metro. But in reality, figuring out which line to take and where to get on and off would be a nightmare.

Fortunately, the information booth has another representation of the same data. It's the Washington Metro map, and it shows all the stations in order on different lines, each shown in a separate color. It also shows where each line intersects, so that you can easily figure out where to switch lines. All of a sudden, navigating the Metro is easy. The subway map doesn't just give you data—it gives you knowledge.

---

1 I was searching for a compelling example of why visualizing information is so important, when I came across the Washington DC metro map in the Infographic page on Wikipedia.

Not only do you know which line to take, but you know roughly how long it'll take to get to your destination. Without much thought you can see that there are eight stops to your destination, stops that are a few minutes apart each, so it'll take a bit more than twenty minutes to get from where you are to the Air and Space Museum. Not only that but you can recognize each of the lines on the Metro not just by its name or final destination, but by its color as well: red, blue, yellow, green, or orange. Each line has a distinct color that you can recognize, both on the map and on the walls of the Metro when you're trying to find the right line to get on.

This simple example illustrates the compelling nature of visualization. With a mix of color, layout, markings, and other elements, a graphic can show us in a few seconds what plain numbers or text might take minutes or hours to convey, if we could draw a conclusion from them at all.

To put things in perspective, the Washington Metro has a mere eighty-six stations. The Tokyo subway, which consists of the Tokyo Metro and the Toei, has some 274 stations. Counting all of the railway networks in the greater Tokyo area, there are some 882 stations in total.[2] That's a lot of stations to try to navigate without a map.

Trend-Spotting

If you've ever used a spreadsheet, you've experienced first-hand how hard it can be to spot trends in a mass of number-filled cells. Unlike in *The Matrix*, where numbers look like images, and images look like numbers, spreadsheets aren't quite as easy to interpret.

---

2 http://en.wikipedia.org/wiki/Tokyo_subway

That's one reason programs like Microsoft Excel and Apple Numbers come with built-in capabilities for creating charts. Often, when we see a graph like a pie or bar chart, it's a lot easier to see how things are changing over time or on a relative basis.

How things change over time is critical when making decisions. A single data point, by itself, is often insufficient to tell us how things are going, regardless of whether we're talking about sales trends or health data.

Investors, for example, often try to evaluate a company's performance. One way to do this is to look at data at a particular moment in time. For example, if a management team were to evaluate the revenue and profits for a given quarter without a view of previous quarters, they might conclude that a company is doing well.

But what that moment-in-time data wouldn't tell the investors was that the company's sales have been growing less and less each quarter. So while sales and profits in the abstract seem to be good, in reality, the company will be headed for bankruptcy if it doesn't find a way to increase sales.

Internal context is one of the key indicators managers and investors use to figure out how business is trending. Mangers and investors also need *external context,* context that tells them how they're doing relative to others.

Suppose that sales are down for a given quarter. Managers might wrongly conclude that their company isn't executing well. In reality, however, sales might be off due to larger industry issues—for example, fewer homes being built in the case of real estate or less travel, in the case of the airline industry. Without external context, that is, data on how other companies in the same industry did over the same period of time, managers have very little insight into what's really causing their business to suffer.

But even when managers have both internal and external context, it's still hard for them to tell what's really going on just by looking at numbers in the abstract. That's where graphics can really help.

Using Visualization To Compress Knowledge

Pictures are worth a thousand words, because, as David McCandless puts it, "Visualization is a form of knowledge compression." One form of compression is reducing the size of data, say by representing a word or a group of words using shorthand, such as a number. But while such compression makes data more efficient to store, it does not make the data easier to understand.

A picture, however, can take a large quantity of information and represent it in a form that's easy to understand. In Big Data, such pictures are referred to as visualization.

Subway maps, pie charts, and bar graphs are all forms of visualization. Although visualization might seem like an easy problem at first, it's hard for a few reasons. First, it's frequently hard to get all the data that people want to visualize into one place and in a consistent format.

Internal and external context data might be stored in two different places. Industry data might be in a market research report, while actual company sales data may be stored in a corporate database. Then, the two forms of data might come in slightly different formats. Company sales data might be stored on a daily basis, while industry data might be available only on a quarterly basis.

Alternatively, the names given to particular pieces of data might be different; a hard drive might be referred to as "Hard Drives" in an industry report but referred to by model number in an internal sales database. Such forms of data inconsistency can make it hard to understand what the data is really telling us.

But by taking all that data and creating a picture of it, the data can become more than data. It can become knowledge.

Visualization is a form of knowledge compression because a seemingly simple image can take vast amounts of structured or un-structured data and compress it down into a few lines and colors that communicate the meaning of all that data quickly and efficiently.

Meet the Leonardo da Vinci of Data

When it comes to data visualization, few people have had as big an impact on the field as Edward Tufte. *The New York Times* called Tufte the Leonardo da Vinci of data.

In 1982, Tufte published one of the defining books of the twen-tieth century, *Visual Display*. Although he began his career teaching courses on political science, Tufte's lifework has been dedicated to the understanding and teaching of information design.

One of Tufte's contributions is a focus on making every piece of data in an illustration matter—and not including any data that doesn't. Tufte's images don't just communicate information; many consider his graphics to be works of art. Visualizations can be useful not only as business tools, Tufte demonstrates; they can also communicate data in a visually appealing way.

Why Is Visual Information So Powerful?

Although it may be difficult to match some of the graphical approaches that Tufte popularized, infographics, as they are now commonly known, have become popular ways to communicate information.

But infographics don't just look good. As with other aspects of Big Data, there is a scientific explanation for what makes visual representations of data so compelling.

In a blog post,[3] Tufte cites a press release about an article published in *Current Biology* that describes just how much information we visually absorb. According to the article, researchers at the University of Pennsylvania School of Medicine estimated that the human retina "can transmit visual input at about the same rate as an Ethernet connection."[4]

For their study, the researchers used an intact retina from a guinea pig combined with a device called a multi-electrode array that measured spikes of electrical impulses from ganglion cells. Ganglion cells carry information from the retina to the brain. Based on their research, the scientists were able to estimate how fast all the ganglion cells—about 100,000 in a pig retina—transmit information. The scientists were then able to calculate how much data the corresponding cells in a human retina transmitted per second. The human retina contains about one million ganglion cells. Put all

---

3 http://www.edwardtufte.com/bboard/q-and-a-fetch-msg?msg_id=0002NC
4 http://www.eurekalert.org/pub_releases/2006-07/uops-prc072606.php

those cells together and the human retina transmits information at about ten megabits per second.

To put that in context, Tor Nørretranders, a Danish popular science author, created a graphic illustrating the bandwidth of our senses. In the graphic, he showed that we receive more information visually than through any of our other senses. If we receive information via sight at about the same rate as a computer network, we receive information through touch at about one tenth that rate, about the rate that a USB key interfaces with a computer.

We receive information through our ears and nose at an even lower rate, about one-tenth of that of touch, or about the same speed at which a hard drive interfaces with a computer; and we receive information through our taste buds at a lower rate still.

In other words, we get information through our eyes at a rate that is ten to a hundred times faster than any of our other senses. So it makes sense that information communicated visually is incredibly powerful. And if that information contains a lot of data compressed into a graphic full of knowledge, we can receive that information even faster.

But that's not the only reason such visual data representations are so powerful. The other reason is that we love to share, and we particularly love to share images.

Images And The Power Of Sharing

On November 22, 2012, users of photo sharing service Instagram shared a lot of photos. It was Instagram's busiest day ever, with users of the service sharing twice the number of photos on that day as they had the day before. That's because November 22 wasn't just any day—it was Thanksgiving. Users of Instagram uploaded some ten million photos that mentioned Thanksgiving-themed words in their captions. To put it mildly, that's a lot of turkey photos, and photos of loved ones too, of course. Some ninety million people now use the service on a monthly basis.[5]

Early in 2012, Facebook purchased Instagram for a billion dollars. Facebook is no slouch either when it comes to sharing photos. Facebook's users were uploading an average of 250 million photos a day as of the end of 2011, or some 7.5 billion photos every month.

There's another reason we love photos, of course, and that is that they are now so easy to take. Just a few short years ago, we had to make decisions about which photos to take and which not to—at the moment the image was available. If we were almost out of film, we might have saved the last shot for another day. But today, digital cameras, smartphones, and cheap storage have made it possible to capture a nearly unlimited number of digital images. Just about every smartphone now has a camera built in. That means that it's possible not only to take all those photos, but to upload and share them easily as well.

Such ease of capturing and sharing images has shown us just how fun and rewarding the activity can be. So it's only natural that when we come across interesting infographics we want to share them too.

And just as with photos, it's a lot easier to create infographics today than it was in the past. There's also more incentive for companies to create such graphics. In February 2011, search engine giant

---

5 http://allthingsd.com/20130117/after-reports-of-user-revolt-instagram-releases-monthly-active-user-data-for-the-first-time/

Google made a change to its algorithms to reward high-quality web-sites, particularly "sites with original content and information such as research, in-depth reports, thoughtful analysis, and so on."[6] As a result, marketers at companies realized they would need to do more in order to get their sites ranked—or listed high—in Google search results.

But what is a marketer with limited information to do in order to create a compelling piece of research? Create an infographic. Infographics can take broad sources of data, mesh them together, and tell a compelling story—stories about the browser wars when it comes to web browsers, or about job creation when it comes to the crowd-funding act. Bloggers and journalists looking for ways to enhance their pieces love such graphics, because readers love to look at and share them.

The most effective infographics don't just get posted online: they get shared, and they get shared repeatedly—some of them go viral, getting shared thousands, or even millions of times on social networks like Twitter, Facebook, and LinkedIn, and through good old e-mail.

As the demand for the creation of infographics has risen, so too have the number of companies and services available to help create them. Visual.ly, a marketplace for creating infographics founded in 2011, lists more than 25,000 infographics in the gallery on its website. Visual.ly will need to show that its business model can scale, but what is clear from the company's gallery is that there is tremendous demand for visual information that communicates a lot of knowledge.

---

6 http://googleblog.blogspot.com/2011/02/finding-more-high-quality-sites-in.html

Other companies such as QlikTech, with its QlikView Product, Tableau Software, and TIBCO with Spotfire provide products that help people create compelling visualizations, for reporting, analysis, and marketing. In 2010, Google introduced Google Public Data Explorer, which lets people explore public data sets online.

Public Datasets

Business users of visualization tools often think of visualization in terms of generating dashboards. Dashboards take data about sales, marketing, and supply chain, and turn that data into meaningful charts that management can review easily.

But the power of visualization extends much further. Public datasets refer to data that is publicly available and frequently collected by governments or government-related organizations. The US Census, first taken in 1790, is one such form of data collection.[7] As a result of the Census, there is a vast amount of information available about the US population, including the composition of the population and its geographic distribution.

As data-storyteller Hans Rosling illustrates, such data is extremely valuable in understanding population changes, the rise and fall of nations, and the progress (or lack thereof) in fighting infant mortality and other epidemics.[8] Rosling uses data visualizations to tell stories with data, in particular public data, in much the way a football commentator uses football replays.

Rosling animates data. He doesn't make cartoons out of it. Rather, he plots data on a graph and then shows how that data changes over

---

7 http://www.census.gov/history/www/census_then_now/
8 http://www.ted.com/talks/hans_rosling_the_good_news_of_the_decade.html

time; how the relative populations or incomes of different nations evolve over periods of forty or fifty years, for example. Such animations bring data to life, and software that Rosling developed with his son and daughter-in-law became the basis for the Google Public Data Explorer.

Some of the most famous visualizations of all time are based on presenting publicly available data in new and compelling ways. Visual.ly showcases a few such charts on its website in a post entitled, "12 Great Visualizations That Made History."[9] Some of these visualizations illustrate just how effective the right graphic can be— John Snow's map of cholera outbreaks in London in 1854 helped explain that water in contaminated wells was responsible for the spread of cholera.

Another famous life-saving chart from around the same time was from Florence Nightingale, known as the mother of modern nursing. Nightingale used a Coxcomb diagram to "convey complex statistical information dramatically to a broad audience."[10] In particular, Nightingale's charts showed that for the British Army, many deaths were preventable: soldiers died from more non-battle causes than battle-related causes. As a result, she was able to convince the government of the importance of using sanitation to decrease mortality rates.

Real Time Visualization

The information most infographics provide is static in nature, and even the animations Rosling created, compelling as they are, are comprised of historical data.

---

9 http://blog.visual.ly/12-great-visualizations-that-made-history/
10 http://www.datavis.ca/gallery/historical.php

Frequently, infographics take a long time and a lot of hard work to create: they require data, an interesting story to tell, and a graphics designer who can present the data in a compelling way. The work doesn't stop there; once the graphic is created, like the tree falling in the woods with no one to hear it, the graphic only has real value if it's distributed, promoted, shared, and viewed. By then of course the data itself may be weeks or months old. So what about presenting compelling visualizations of data that is real-time in nature?

For data to be valuable in real time, three things must happen. The data itself must be available, there must be sufficient storage and computer processing power to store and analyze the data, and there must be a compelling way to visualize the data that doesn't require days or weeks of work.

If the idea of knowing what millions of people think about something in real-time, and being able to visually illustrate what they think seems far-fetched, it isn't. We need look no further than the 2012 presidential election to see why.

In decades past, polling was performed by individual pollsters calling people to ask their opinions or talking to them in person. By combining polls of a relatively small number of people with statistical sampling methods, pollsters were able to make predictions about the outcome of elections and draw conclusions about how people felt about important political issues.

Nielsen used similar forms of statistics for television measurement, and Comscore did the same for the web. Nielsen originally performed media measurement by using a device to detect to which stations a thousand people had tuned their radios.[11] The company

---

11 http://en.wikipedia.org/wiki/Nielsen_Company

later applied a related approach to television shows in what became widely known as Nielsen ratings.

Such forms of measurement are still widely used, but as in other areas, Big Data is transforming the way we do measurement. If there is one company in the last few years that has had more impact on our ability to measure public opinion than any other—an activity known as sentiment analysis—it is Twitter.

In fact, Twitter may be one of the most under-appreciated companies around in terms of its Big Data assets. As of October 2012, Twitter users were sending some five hundred million tweets—short text messages—across the network per day,[12] a remarkable amount of human-generated information. That's up from no tweets sent at all in 2006.

By evaluating the words used in tweets, computer programs can not only detect which topics are trending—that is, receiving more attention—but also draw conclusions about how people feel and what opinions they hold.

Capturing and storing such data is just one aspect of the kind of Big Data challenge and opportunity a company like Twitter faces. To make it possible to analyze such data, the company has to provide access to the stream of tweets, that is, nearly five thousand text messages per second, and even more during events like presidential debates, when users create some twenty thousand tweets per second. Then comes the task of analyzing those tweets for common words, and finally, presenting all that data visually.

---

12 http://news.cnet.com/8301-1023_3-57541566-93/report-twitter-hits-half-a-billion-tweets-a-day/

Handling such massive, real-time streams of data is difficult, but not impossible. Twitter itself provides programmatic interfaces to what is commonly known as the firehose of tweets. Around Twitter, companies like Gnip have emerged to provide access as well.

Other companies, such as BrightContext, provide tools for real-time sentiment analysis; during the 2012 presidential debates, the *Washington Post* used BrightContext's real-time sentiment module to measure and chart sentiment while viewers watched the debates.[13] Topsy, a real-time search company that has indexed some two hundred billion tweets, powered Twitter's political index, known as the Twindex. Vizzuality specializes in mapping geospatial data and powered the *Wall Street Journal*'s election maps.

In contrast to phone-based polling, which is time-consuming and typically costs around twenty dollars per interview, real-time measurement simply costs compute cycles and can be done on an unprecedented scale. Products like those from some of the companies mentioned here can then provide real-time visualization of the data collected.

But real-time visualization doesn't stop at displaying real-time information in websites. Google Glass,[14] which *Time Magazine* called one of the best inventions of 2012, is "a computer built into the frame of a pair of glasses, and it's the device that will make augmented reality part of our daily lives."[15] In the future, not only will we be able to see visual representations of data on our comput-

---

13 http://www.forbes.com/sites/davefeinleib/2012/10/22/not-your-grandmothers-presidential-debate/5/

14 http://www.forbes.com/sites/davefeinleib/2012/10/17/3-big-data-insights-from-the-grandfather-of-google-glass/

15 http://techland.time.com/2012/11/01/best-inventions-of-the-year-2012/slide/google-glass/

ers and mobile phones, we'll also be able to visualize—and understand—the physical world better as we move around it.

If that sounds like something out of a science fiction book, it's not. Today, Google Glass costs $1,500 and is somewhat bulky. But just as other new technologies have gotten smaller and cheaper over time, so too will Google Glass.

Why Understanding Images Is Easy For Us And Hard For Computers

Ironically, while computers excel at processing large amounts of textual information, they still struggle with analyzing visual information. Just recall the last time you took a few hundred photos and wished you had a website or a piece of software that would automatically weed out the bad photos and group related photos together; or that could automatically figure out who is in the photos and share copies of those photos with those people

On a larger scale, companies like Facebook have to filter out inappropriate images from good ones. Amazon has to determine which textual product descriptions match their image counterparts, and which ones don't. These would seem to be relatively easy problems for computers to solve, and yet, while the science of image recognition and characterization has advanced significantly, performing such analysis at large scale remains challenging. In fact, human beings perform many of these recognition and matching tasks.

In their paper, *Why is Real-World Visual Object Recognition Hard?*,[16] scientists from MIT and Harvard stated, "The ease with

16 http://www.ploscompbiol.org/article/info:doi/10.1371/journal.pcbi.0040027

which we recognize visual objects belies the computational difficulty of this feat. At the core of this challenge is image variation—any given object can cast an infinite number of different images onto the retina, depending on an object's position, size, orientation, pose, lighting, etc."

Simply put, images can have a lot of variability, making it difficult to tell when different images contain the same objects or people. What's more, pattern detection is more difficult; while the word "president" is easy to find in a sentence, and hence relatively easy to find in millions of sentences, it's much harder to recognize the person holding that title in images.

Having an individual human being characterize images is one thing. But what about trying to do it with millions of images? To solve their image characterization problems, companies like Amazon and Facebook turn to crowd-sourcing marketplaces like oDesk and Amazon Mechanical Turk.[17] On these marketplaces, content moderators who pass certain tests or meet certain qualifications gain access to images and can then characterize and filter them.

Today, computers are good at helping us create visualizations. But tomorrow, as products like Google Glass continue to evolve, they may also help us better understand visual information in real time.

The Psychology and Physiology Of Visualization

If there's one industry that understands the importance of presenting information visually better than any other, it's the advertising industry. The advertising industry is one of several that are on the leading edge of taking advantage of new Big Data technologies.

---

17 http://gawker.com/5885714/

If there is any doubt that images are powerful means of communication, we need look no further than the $70 billion US companies spend each year on TV advertising.[18] As Nigel Hollis, chief global analyst at market-research firm Millward Brown points out, companies wouldn't spend so much on TV advertising if it didn't work.[19]

Where people get confused about the impact of TV advertising, Hollis says, is in thinking that advertisers want to get them to do something immediately. That's where they're wrong. Brand advertising doesn't succeed through calls to action or arguments, but rather through leaving positive impressions. Hollis explains, "The best advertisements use images, jingles, and stories to focus attention on the brand." In particular, says Hollis, "engaging and memorable ads slip ideas past our defenses and seed memories that influence our behavior."

In fact, some advertisers have taken the delivery of visual images one step further, applying data analysis to determine which visualizations are most effective through a science called neuromarketing. Neuromarketing uses functional magnetic resonance imaging (fMRI) and other technologies "to observe which areas of the brain 'light up'"[20] in response to a variety of advertising approaches. Marketers can even simulate situations to determine which placement—such as on billboards or on the sides of buses—produces the most impact.

Thus visualization is not only an effective way to communicate large quantities of data, but it also ties directly into the brain,

---

18 http://www.theatlantic.com/business/archive/2011/08/why-good-advertising-works-even-when-you-think-it-doesnt/244252/

19 Post on *The Atlantic* entitled "Why Good Advertising Works (Even When You Think It Doesn't)"

20 http://www.businessweek.com/stories/2007-10-08/this-is-your-brain-on-advertisingbusinessweek-business-news-stock-market-and-financial-advice

triggering emotional and chemical responses. Visualization may be one of the most effective ways to communicate a data-based message. What studies have shown is that it is not just the visualization itself that matters, but when, where, and how such visualizations are presented.

By setting the right context, choosing the right colors, even selecting the right time of day, it's possible to communicate the insights locked up in vast amounts of data a lot more effectively. As the famous media researcher Marshall McLuhan once said, "The medium is the message." Now scientific evidence is showing just how important context and delivery is when communicating information.

The Visualization Multiplier Effect

As we've seen in this chapter, visualization and data go hand in hand. There are instances, of course, where computers can act on data with no human involvement. For example, it simply wouldn't be possible for humans to figure out which text ads to display alongside search results when dealing with the billions of search queries we make. Similarly, computer systems excel at automated pricing decisions and evaluating millions of transactions quickly to determine which ones are fraudulent.

But there remain any number of situations in which we as humans are trying to make better decisions based on data. Just because we have more data available does not mean that it's easier to produce better insights from that data.

In fact, the opposite may be true. The more data we have, the more important it becomes to be able to distill that data into meaningful insights that we can act on. Visualizing such data may be one of the most powerful mechanisms we have for doing so.

Visualization is effective because (as we saw earlier) our eyes have ultra-high throughput into our brains—as much as a hundred times greater than some of our other senses. Visualization can take the facts—the data—and trigger emotional responses. It can compress vast amounts of data into knowledge we can use.

Combine the knowledge compression of visualization with the high throughput of visual delivery, and you get the visualization multiplier effect—more data absorbed faster.

Big Data isn't just about the data itself, but about how we communicate it, and what we do with it. Big Data also isn't just the domain of scientists, data analysts, or engineers—data is everywhere, all around us, from the charts we see to the advertisements that bombard us on our way to work.

Social media platforms are changing the way we communicate, and enabling the broader distribution not just of textual information, but also of high-impact visual knowledge. With the right visualization, data is more than just text or numbers.

The right visualization can tell a story that has a very real impact, not just in business but in broader contexts such as global health as well.

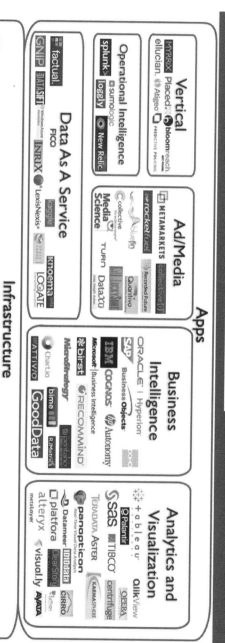

THE BIG DATA LANDSCAPE

Apps

Vertical
ellucian. • bloomreach • Atigeo • PREDICTIVE POLICING
MYRRIX Placed • MetaMarkets

Operational Intelligence
splunk> • sumologic
loggly • New Relic

Ad/Media
METAMARKETS • SocialFlow [V]
rocketfuel
collective
bluefin • Quantivo
Media Science • TURN • DataXu
Recorded Future

Business Intelligence
ORACLE | Hyperion
SAP Business Objects
IBM COGNOS • Autonomy
birst • Business Intelligence • RECOMMND
MicroStrategy
Chart.io • bime • pentaho
Attivio • GoodData • Jaspersoft

Analytics and Visualization
tableau • Palantir
SAS • TIBCO • centrifuge • QlikView
TERADATA ASTER • KARMASPHERE • OPERA
panopticon
Datameer • metamarkets • CIRRO
platfora • visual.ly • AYATA
alteryx • metalayer

Infrastructure

Analytics
Hortonworks • VERTICA
cloudera • INFOBRIGHT • ParAccel • MAPR
EMC² • GREENPLUM
(N) NETEZZA
DATASTAX • kognitio • pervasive

Data As A Service
FICO
GNIP • DATASIFT • WindowsAzure
factual • INRIX • LexisNexis • gnip
Knoema • LOQATE

Operational
COUCHBASE • 10gen | MongoDB
AEROSPIKE • HADAPT
TERRACOTTA • VoltDB
MarkLogic • informatica

As A Service
Qubole • Windows Azure
amazon web services
infochimps • MORTAR
Google BigQuery

Structured DB
ORACLE
IBM • SQL Server • DB2
PostgreSQL
memsql • MySQL • SYBASE
TERADATA

Chapter Five

The Big Data Landscape

Now that we've explored a few aspects of Big Data, we'll take a look at the broader landscape of companies that are playing a role in the Big Data ecosystem. When it comes to the Big Data Landscape, it's easiest to think about it in terms of infrastructure and applications.

The chart that follows is the Big Data Landscape, April 2013 edition. The Landscape categorizes many of the players in the Big Data space. Since new entrants are always emerging, the latest version of the Landscape is available on the web at www.bigdatalandscape.com.

Infrastructure is primarily responsible for storing and to some extent processing the immense amounts of data that companies are capturing. Applications are what humans or computer systems use to gain insights from data.

People use applications to visualize data so they can make better decisions, while computer systems use applications to serve up the right ads to the right people, or to detect credit card fraud, among other activities. Although we can't touch on every company in the landscape, we will describe a number of them and examine how the ecosystem came to be.

Market Growth

Market-research firm IDC expects the Big Data market to grow to $16.9 billion by 2015, and that the growth rate in the space will be 40 percent annually, or about seven times that of other information technology areas.[1] Another research firm, Wikibon, notes that pure-play Big Data vendors accounted for only $468 million in revenue in 2011. Although that's a relatively small percentage of the total revenue in the space, Wikibon believes that these pure-play vendors have been a major source of innovation.

The amount of data we're generating is growing at an astounding rate. One of the most interesting measures of this is Facebook's growth. In October 2012, the company announced it had hit one billion users—nearly 15 percent of the world's population. Facebook had to develop a variety of new technologies to keep up with this immense growth in users.

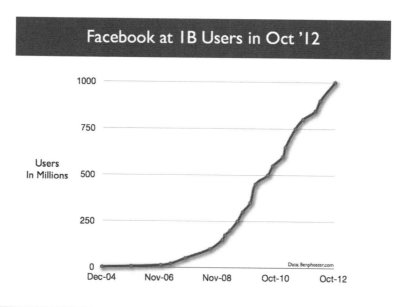

1 http://www.cioinsight.com/c/a/Latest-News/Big-Data-Market-to-Grow-to-169-Billion-by-2015-IDC-118144/

Facebook handles 2.7 billion Likes, 2.5 billion shared-content items, and three hundred million photo uploads every day. That means the company stores more than a hundred petabytes when it comes to the data it uses for analytics, and ingests more than five hundred terabytes of new data per day.[2] That's the equivalent of adding the data stored on roughly two thousand Macintosh Air hard drives, if they were all fully used.

Twitter provides another interesting measure of data growth. The company reached more than five hundred million registered users as of 2012 and handling more than five hundred million tweets per day, up from twenty thousand per day just five years earlier.

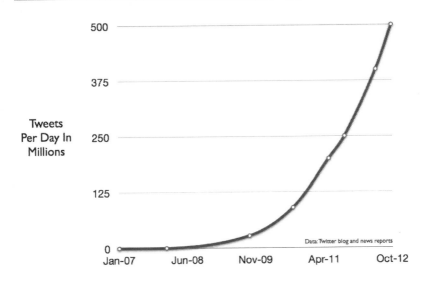

Twitter at 500M Tweets Per Day in Oct '12

2 http://us.gizmodo.com/5937143/what-facebook-deals-with-everyday-27-billion-likes-300-million-photos-uploaded-and-500-terabytes-of-data

To put this in perspective, however, this is just the data that human beings generate. Machines are generating even more data. Every time we click on a website button, make a purchase, call someone on the phone, or do virtually any other activity, we leave a digital trail. The simple action of uploading a photo generates lots of other data: who uploaded the photo and when, whom was it shared with, what tags are associated with it, and so on.

The volume of data is growing all around us: Walmart handles more than a million customer transactions every hour and about ninety trillion e-mails are sent every year. Ironically, almost three-quarters of all that e-mail, 71.8 percent of it, is considered spam.[3] According to IBM, 90 percent of the data in the world today was created in just the last two years. And the volume of business data doubles every 1.2 years, according to one estimate.[4]

To address this incredible growth, a number of new companies have emerged, and a number of existing companies are repositioning themselves and their offerings around Big Data.

The Role of Open Source

Open source has played a large role in the recent evolution of Big Data. But before we talk about that, it's important to provide some context on the role of open source more generally.

Just a few years ago, Linux became a mainstream operating system, and in combination with commodity hardware (low-cost, off-the-shelf servers) cannibalized once-dominant vendors like Sun

---

3 http://www.securelist.com/en/analysis/204792243/Spam_in_July_2012
4 http://knowwpcarey.com/article.cfm?cid=25&aid=1171

Microsystems. Sun, for example, was well known for its version of Unix, called Solaris, which ran on its custom SPARC hardware.

With Linux, enterprises were able to use an open-source operating system on low-cost hardware to get much of the same functionality, at a much lower cost. The availability of MySQL, an open-source database, the Apache open-source web server, and PHP, an open-source scripting language originally created for building websites, also drove the popularity of Linux.

As enterprises began to use and adopt Linux for large-scale commercial use, they required enterprise-grade support and reliability. It was fine for engineers to work with open-source Linux in the lab, but businesses needed a vendor they could call on for training, support, and customization. Put another way, big companies like buying from other big companies.

Among a number of vendors, Red Hat emerged as the market leader in delivering commercial support and service for Linux. The company now has a market cap of just over $10 billion. MySQL AB, a Swedish company, sponsored the development of the open source MySQL database project. Sun Microsystems acquired MySQL AB for $1 billion in early 2008, and Oracle acquired Sun in late 2009.

Both IBM and Oracle, among others, commercialized large-scale relational databases. Relational databases allow data to be stored in well-defined tables and accessed by a key. For example, an employee might be identified by an employee number, and that number would then be associated with a number of other fields containing information about the employee—her name, address, hire date, position, and so on.

Such databases worked well until companies had to contend with really large quantities of unstructured data. Google had to deal with huge numbers of web pages and the relationships between links in those pages. Facebook had to contend with social-graph data. The social graph is the digital representation of the relationships between people on its social network—and all of the unstructured data at the end of each point in the graph, such as photos, messages, profiles, and the like. Such companies also wanted to take advantage of the lower costs of commodity hardware.

So companies like Google, Yahoo, Facebook, and others developed their own solutions for storing and processing vast quantities of data. Just as open-source versions of Unix and databases like Oracle emerged in the form of Linux and MySQL, much the same thing is happening in the Big Data world.

Apache Hadoop, an open-source distributed computing platform for storing large quantities of data via the Hadoop Distributed File System (HDFS), and dividing operations on that data into small fragments via a programming model called MapReduce, was derived from technologies originally built at Google. A related set of open-source technologies have emerged around Hadoop.

Apache Hive provides data-warehousing capabilities including data-extract/transform/load (ETL), a process for extracting data from a variety of sources, transforming it to fit operational needs (including ensuring the quality of the data), and loading it into the target database.[5] Apache HBase provides real-time read-write access to very large structured tables on top of Hadoop. It is modeled on Google's BigTable. Meanwhile, Apache Cassandra, by replicating data, provides fault-tolerant data storage.

Historically, such capabilities were only available from commercial software vendors, typically on specialized hardware. Linux

---

5 http://en.wikipedia.org/wiki/Extract,_transform,_load

made the capabilities of Unix available on commodity hardware, drastically reducing the cost of computing. In much the same way, open-source Big Data technologies are making data storage and processing capabilities that were only available to companies like Google, or from commercial vendors, available on commodity hardware.

This reduces the up-front cost of working with Big Data, and has the potential to make Big Data accessible to a much larger number of potential users. Closed-source vendors point out that while open-source software is free to adopt, it can be costly to maintain, especially at scale.

That said, the fact that open-source is free to start using has made it an appealing option to many. Some commercial vendors have adopted freemium business models to compete. Products are free to use on a personal basis or for a limited amount of data, but customers are required to pay for departmental or larger data usage.

Those enterprises that adopt open-source technologies over time tend to require commercial support for them, much as they did with Linux. Companies like Cloudera, HortonWorks, and MapR are addressing that need for Hadoop, while companies like DataStax are doing the same for Cassandra, and LucidWorks is performing such as role for Apache Lucerne, an open-source text search engine used for indexing and searching large quantities of web pages or documents.

Enter The Cloud

Yet two other market trends are occurring in parallel. First, the volume of data is increasing—doubling almost every year. We are generating more data in the form of photos, tweets, likes, and e-mails; our data has data associated with it; and machines generate data in the form of status updates and other information from servers, cars, airplanes, mobile phones, and other devices. As a result, the complexity of working with all that data is increasing. More data means more data to integrate, understand, and to milk for insights. It also means higher risks around data security and data privacy. And while companies historically viewed internal data (such as sales figures) and external data (like brand sentiment or market-research numbers) separately, they now want to integrate those kinds of data, to take advantage of the resulting insights.

Second, enterprises are moving computing and processing to the cloud. This means that instead of buying hardware and software, installing it in their own data centers, and then maintaining that infrastructure, they're now getting the capabilities they want on-demand over the Internet. Software as a Service (SaaS) company Salesforce.com pioneered the delivery of applications over the web with its "no software" model for customer relationship management (CRM). The company has continued to build an ecosystem of offerings to complement its core CRM solution.

Meanwhile, Amazon paved the way for infrastructure on demand—computing and storage in the cloud with Amazon Web Services (AWS). Amazon launched AWS[6] in 2003 with the idea that it could make a profit on the infrastructure required to run the Amazon.com store.[7] The company has continued to add on-demand infrastructure services that allow developers to bring up new servers, storage, and databases quickly.

Amazon has also introduced Big Data-specific services including Amazon MapReduce, an Amazon cloud-based version of the open

---

6 http://phx.corporate-ir.net/phoenix.zhtml?c=176060&p=irol-corporateTimeline

7 http://en.wikipedia.org/wiki/Amazon_Web_Services#cite_note-1

source Hadoop-MapReduce offering. Amazon RedShift is a data-warehousing on-demand solution that Amazon expects will cost as little as $1,000 per terabyte per year—less than a tenth of what companies typically pay for on-premise data-warehousing, which can run more than $20,000 per terabyte annually.[8] Meanwhile, Amazon Glacier provides low-cost digital archiving services at $0.01 per gigabyte per month, or about $120 per terabyte per year.

Amazon has two primary advantages over other providers. It has a very well-known consumer brand. It also benefits from the economies of scale it gets from supporting the Amazon.com website, as well as from serving so many other customers on its infrastructure. Other well-known companies also offer cloud infrastructure, including Google with its Google Cloud Platform, and Microsoft with Windows Azure, but Amazon has paved the way and grabbed pole position with AWS.

The advantage of all of these cloud services over traditional offerings is that customers pay only for what they use. This is especially beneficial for startups, which can avoid the expensive up-front costs typically associated with buying, deploying, and managing server and storage infrastructure.

AWS has seen incredible growth. The service was expected to bring in $1.5 billion in revenue for the company in 2012.[9] As of June 2012, Amazon was storing more than a trillion objects in its Simple Storage Service (S3) and was adding more than forty thousand new objects per second.[10] That number is up from just 2.9 billion objects

---

8 http://www.informationweek.com/software/information-management/amazon-redshift-leaves-on-premises-openi/240143912

9 http://www.theage.com.au/it-pro/cloud/amazon-apologises-for-christmas-eve-outage-20130101-2c3q6.html

10 http://aws.typepad.com/aws/2012/06/amazon-s3-the-first-trillion-objects.html

stored as of the end of 2006, and 262 billion at the end of 2010. Companies like Netflix, Dropbox, and others run their businesses on AWS.

The company continues to broaden its on-demand infrastructure offerings, adding services for IP routing, e-mail sending, and a host of Big Data related services. Amazon also works with an ecosystem of partners to offer their infrastructure products as well. Thus, the headline for any new infrastructure start-up thinking about building a public cloud offering may well be the following: find a way to partner with Amazon or expect the company to come out with a competitive offering.

Overcoming The Challenges Of The Cloud

Of course, many are still skeptical of taking advantage of public cloud infrastructure. Historically there have been three major potential issues with such services. First, enterprises felt that such services were not secure. In-house infrastructure was believed to be more secure. Second, many large vendors simply didn't offer Internet/cloud versions of their software. Companies had to buy the hardware and run the software themselves or hire a third party to do so. Finally, it was difficult to get large volumes of data from in-house systems into the cloud.

While the first challenge remains true for certain government agencies, companies like Salesforce.com have proven that they can securely store the confidential data of many companies. Businesses are accepting more applications delivered over the net.

The market values Workday, a web-based provider of HR management solutions, at nearly $10.5 billion. First it was customer data, then HR data. Over time, more and more line-of-business functions will migrate their data to the cloud.

The third challenge, moving massive amounts of data to the cloud, remains an issue. Many experts feel that when it comes to really high volume data, data that starts on-premise, at a company, will remain there, while data that starts in the cloud will stay there.

But as more line-of-business applications become available over the net, more data will start in the cloud, and more data will stay there. In addition, companies are emerging to provide technologies that speed up the transfer of large quantities of data. Aspera, for example, has focused on accelerating file-transfer speeds, particularly for large audio and video files. Companies like Netflix use Aspera to transfer files at up to ten times traditional speeds.

With the cloud, companies get a host of other advantages: they spend less time maintaining and deploying hardware and software, and they can scale on-demand. If a company needs more computing resources or storage, that's not a matter of months but of minutes. What's more, enterprises with installed software have traditionally lagged behind in terms of using the latest version of the software. With applications that come over the net, users can be on the latest version as soon as it's available.

Of course, there are trade-offs. Companies are at the cost-mercy of the public cloud provider they choose to work with. But competition between cloud vendors has continued to push prices down.

Customers also depend on such providers to deliver reliable service. Amazon has suffered a few major high-profile outages that have caused some to question whether relying on its service makes sense. One such outage caused movie-streaming provider Netflix to lose service on Christmas Eve and Christmas Day 2012, traditionally a very popular time for watching movies.

As Amazon and other providers continue to introduce more infrastructure-on-demand capabilities—and as those providers continue to compete with each other and reduce prices—it's likely that more companies will continue to take advantage of such services.

Infrastructure

With the context of open source and Big Data in the cloud in mind, we'll now take a look at some of the companies playing key roles in the infrastructure and applications spaces.

In the larger context, venture investors have put a relatively small amount of capital to work in Big Data infrastructure, with investments in Hadoop-related companies (Cloudera, HortonWorks, MapR) and NoSQL companies (10Gen, Aerospike, Couchbase, and others) totaling less than $500 million.

Cloudera has been perhaps the most visible of all of the new Big Data infrastructure companies. Cloudera sells tools and consulting services that help companies run Hadoop. As of December 2012, the company had raised $140 million in venture capital from Accel Partners, Greylock Partners, Meritech Capital Partners, In-Q-Tel, and Ignition Partners.[11] Cloudera was founded by Mike Olson, Amr Awadallah, who had worked with Hadoop at Yahoo, Jeff Hammerbacher, who had worked with it at Facebook, and Christophe Bisciglia from Google.[12]

---

11 The author is an investor in Ignition Partners.

12 http://www.xconomy.com/san-francisco/2010/11/04/is-cloudera-the-next-oracle-ceo-mike-olson-hopes-so/2/

It is interesting to note that Google first published a paper describing Google MapReduce and Google File System, from which Hadoop is derived, in 2004.[13] That goes to show just how long it takes for technologies used in large consumer companies like Google to make their way into the enterprise.

Cloudera competitor HortonWorks was spun out of Yahoo!. Its engineers have contributed more than 80 percent of the code for Apache Hadoop. MapR focuses on delivering a higher-performance version of Hadoop with its M5 offering, which tries to address the biggest knock on Hadoop: the long time it takes to process data.

At the same time as these companies are delivering and supporting Hadoop in the enterprise, other companies are emerging to deliver Hadoop in the cloud. Qubole, Nodeable, and Platfora are three companies in the cloud-Hadoop space. The challenge for these companies will be standing out from native Big Data cloud-processing offerings such as Amazon's own MapReduce offering.

Hadoop was designed to perform batch-based operations across very large datasets, where engineers design jobs, the jobs are spread across hundreds or thousands of servers, and the individual results are then pulled back together to produce the actual result. As a very simple example, a Hadoop MapReduce job might be used to count the number of occurrences of words in various documents. If there were millions of documents, that would be difficult to do on a single machine. Hadoop breaks the jobs into smaller pieces that each machine can perform, and then the results of each individual counting job are added together to produce the final count.

---

13 http://static.googleusercontent.com/external_content/untrusted_dlcp/
research.google.com/en/us/archive/mapreduce-osdi04.pdf

The challenge is that running such jobs can consume a lot of time—which is not ideal for querying data in real time. New additions to Hadoop, such as the Cloudera Impala project, promise to make Hadoop more responsive, not just for batch processing, but for near real-time analytics applications as well.[14] Of course, such innovations also make Cloudera a desirable acquisition target (before or after going public) for an existing, large analytics or data-warehousing provider—IBM, Oracle, and others are all potential buyers. Meanwhile, EMC introduced its Pivotal Hadoop Distribution (Pivotal HD) in February 2013.

Applications

Most of us use Big Data Applications (BDAs) every day. Facebook, Google, LinkedIn, Netflix, Pandora, and Twitter are just a few of the many applications that use large amounts of data to give us insights and keep us entertained.

While we'll continue to see innovation in Big Data infrastructure, much of the interest going forward in Big Data will be in BDAs that take advantage of the vast amounts of data being generated, and the low-cost computing power available to process it.

Facebook stores and uses Big Data in the form of user profiles, photos, messages, and advertisements. By analyzing such data, the company is better able to understand its users and figure out what content to show them.

Google crawls billions of web pages and has a vast array of other Big Data sources such as Google Maps, which contains an immense

---

14 http://blog.cloudera.com/blog/2012/10/cloudera-impala-real-time-queries-in-apache-hadoop-for-real/

amount of data—not just about physical street locations, but also satellite imagery, on-street photos, and even inside views of many buildings.

Meanwhile, LinkedIn hosts millions of online resumes, as well as the knowledge about how people are connected to each other. Out of hundreds of millions of people, the company is able to use all that data to suggest people with whom we might want to connect.

Internet-radio service Pandora uses some four hundred song attributes to figure out what songs to recommend. The company employs musicologists who characterize the attributes of virtually every new song that comes out and store its characteristics as part of the Music Genome Project.[15] As of October 2011, the company had in its database more than nine hundred thousand songs from more than ninety thousand artists.

In a similar vein, Netflix is well known for its movie-prediction algorithms, which enable it to suggest to viewers what movie to watch next. The company relies on a group of about forty human taggers to makes notes on more than a hundred attributes—from storyline to tone—that define each movie.[16]

Twitter handles more than five hundred million tweets per day. Now, companies like Topsy, a data-analytics startup that performs real-time analysis of tweets, are using such data sources to build applications on top of Twitter and other platforms.

Such applications are a sign of things to come, especially for businesses. Enterprises have historically built and maintained their

---

15 http://www.time.com/time/magazine/article/0,9171,1992403,00.html
16 http://consumerist.com/2012/07/09/how-does-netflix-categorize-movies/

own infrastructure for processing Big Data and in many cases developed custom applications for analyzing that data. All that is starting to change in a variety of areas, from online advertising to operational intelligence.

Online Advertising Applications

To determine which ad to show you, companies use algorithmic solutions to process huge volumes of data in real time. Based on this automated analysis, they are able to figure out which ad is most relevant to you and how much to pay (or charge) for particular ad impressions. Vendors in this space include Collective, DataXu, Metamarkets, Rocket Fuel, Turn, and a number of others.

The Rocket Fuel platform handled some thirteen billion queries per day as of June 2012. The Turn platform processes some thirty billion advertising decisions and 1.5 trillion customer attributes daily. Meanwhile, AdMeld (now part of Google) works with publishers to help them optimize their ad inventory.

Instead of providing just basic ad serving, these companies use advanced algorithms to analyze a variety of attributes across a range of data sources to optimize ad delivery.

Marketers will continue to shift more dollars to online advertising, which suggests that this category is likely to witness both growth and consolidation. Mobile advertising and mobile analytics present one of the largest potential growth areas, because of the amount of time consumers and business users now spend on mobile devices.

Companies like Flurry provide analytics capabilities that allow mobile-app developers to measure consumer behavior and monetize their audiences more effectively. At the same time, the mobile area is also one of the most complex due to the amount of control that Google, Apple, and hardware vendors like Samsung exert in the space.

Sales and Marketing Applications

Salesforce.com changed the way companies did Customer Relationship Management (CRM) by introducing its "no software" hosted model for CRM, as an alternative to PeopleSoft and other offerings that had to be run on-premise. More recently, marketing automation companies like Eloqua (now a part of Oracle), Marketo, and Hubspot have systematized the way companies do lead management, demand generation, and e-mail marketing.

But today's marketers face a new set of challenges. They have to manage and understand customer campaigns and interactions across a large number of channels.

Today's marketers need to ensure that a company is optimizing its web pages so they get indexed in Google and Bing and are easy for potential customers to find. Marketers need to ensure a regular presence on social media channels such as Facebook, Twitter, and Google Plus. This is not just because these are venues where people are spending time getting entertainment and information, but also because of Google's stronger emphasis on social media as a way to gauge the importance of a particular piece of content.

As Patrick Moran, vice president of marketing at application performance monitoring company New Relic points out, marketers also need to factor in a variety of other sources of data to understand their customers fully. This includes actual product usage data, lead sources, and trouble ticket information. Such data can give marketers significant insight into which customers are most valuable—so they can look for other potential customers with similar attributes—and what activities are most likely to result in prospects converting.

All of this means a lot of data for marketers to visualize and act on. As Brian Kardon, chief marketing officer of Lattice Engines and formerly of Eloqua and Forrester Research, suggests, marketing in the future will be in large part about algorithms.[17] Trading on Wall Street was once the purview of humans, until computer-run algorithmic trading took its place. Kardon envisions a similar future for marketing, a future in which algorithms analyze all of these data sources to find useful patterns and tell marketers what to do next.

Such software will likely tell marketers which campaigns to run, which e-mails to send, what blog posts to write, and when and what to tweet. It won't stop there, however.

Ultimately Big Data marketing applications will not only analyze all these data sources, but also perform much of the work to optimize campaigns based on the data. Companies like BloomReach are already heading down this path with algorithm-based software that helps e-commerce companies optimize their websites for highest conversion.

Of course, the creative part of marketing will remain critical, and marketers will still have to make the big-picture decisions about where to invest and how to position. But BDAs for marketing will play a significant role in automating much of the manual work currently associated with online marketing.

---

17 http://www.b2bmarketinginsider.com/strategy/real-time-marketing-trading-room-floor

Visualization Applications

As access to data becomes more democratized, visualization becomes ever more important. There are many companies in the visualization space, so in this section we'll highlight just a few of them. Tableau Software is well known for its interactive and easy-to-use visualization software. The company's technology came out of research at Stanford University. As of this writing, industry insiders project the company is well on its way to reaching $100 million in annual revenue, and an IPO is expected soon.

QlikTech offers its popular QlikView visualization product, which some twenty-six thousand companies use around the world. The company went public in 2010 and is valued at just under $2.4 billion as of March 2013. TIBCO offers its Spotfire visualization and analytics product.

While not strictly a visualization company, Palantir is well known for its Big Data software and has a strong customer base in government and financial services. There are also offerings from large-enterprise vendors including IBM, Microsoft, Oracle, SAP, and SAS.

More and more companies are adding tools for embedding interactive visualizations into websites. Publishers now use such visualizations to provide readers greater insights into data.

Enterprise collaboration and social networking companies, like Jive Software and Yammer, emerged to make business communication—both externally and internally—more social. Expect to see similar social capabilities become a standard part of nearly every data analytics and visualization offering.

Given the importance of visualization as a way to understand large data sets and complex relationships, new tools will continue to emerge. The challenge and opportunity for such tools is not just to help humans make better decisions, but to apply algorithms (or at least to help in the development of algorithms) that automate decisions that don't require human involvement.

Business Intelligence Applications

Much of the history of data analysis has been in business intelligence (BI). Organizations rely on BI to organize and analyze large quantities of corporate data with the goal of helping managers make better decisions. For example, by analyzing sales and supply chain data, managers might be able to decide on better pricing approaches in the future.

Business Intelligence was first referenced in a 1958 article by an IBM researcher[18] and the company has continued to break new ground with technical advances like algorithmic trading and IBM Watson. Other major vendors, including SAP, SAS, and Oracle all offer business intelligence products. MicroStrategy remains an independent player in the space. It has a market cap of about a billion dollars and has recently introduced compelling mobile offerings to the market.

Domo, a cloud-based, business-intelligence software company, is a relatively recent entry into the market. Domo was founded by Josh James, the former founder and CEO of analytics-leader Omniture (now Adobe). Other well-known players in the space include GoodData and Birst. The hosted BI space has proven difficult to crack due to the challenge of getting companies to move critical company data into the cloud, but as with other areas, that is starting to change.

---

18 http://en.wikipedia.org/wiki/Business_intelligence

Operational Intelligence

By performing searches and looking at charts, companies are able to understand the cause of server failures and other infrastructure issues. Rather than building their own scripts and software to understand infrastructure failures, enterprises are starting to rely on newer operational intelligence companies like Splunk. The company provides both on-premise and cloud-based versions of its software, which IT engineers use to analyze the vast amounts of log data that servers, networking equipment, and other devices generate. Splunk also serves use cases that span security and compliance, application management, web intelligence, and business analytics.

Sumo Logic and Loggly are more recent entrants in the space, and large vendors such as TIBCO (which acquired LogLogic) and HP (which acquired ArcSight), and existing player Vitria, have offerings as well.

Data As A Service

One category that straddles Big Data infrastructure and applications is Data as a Service (DaaS). Historically, companies have had to obtain Big Data sets and then work with them—it was often hard to get current data or to get it over the Internet. Now, however, DaaS providers come in a variety of forms. Dun & Bradstreet provides web-programming interfaces for financial, address, and other forms of data. FICO offers financial information. Twitter offers access to its tweet streams.

Such data sources allow others to build interesting applications based on them—applications that can accurately predict the outcomes of presidential elections or understand how consumers feel about a brand. There are also companies that provide vertical, specific DaaS: BlueKai provides data related to consumer profiles, Inrix provides traffic data, and LexisNexis provides legal data.

Data Cleansing

Perhaps one of the most unglamorous yet critical areas when it comes to working with data is that of data cleansing and integration. Companies like Informatica have long played a role in this space. Internal and external data can be stored in wide range of formats and can include errors and duplicate records. Such data often needs to be cleansed before it can be used, or before multiple data sources can be used together.

At its simplest level, data cleansing involves tasks like removing duplicate records and normalizing address fields. Going forward, it's quite possible we'll see data cleansing available as a cloud-based service.

Data Privacy

As we move more data to the cloud and publish more information about ourselves on the net, data privacy remains a growing concern. Even data that seems anonymous often isn't. In one study, analysts were able to look at anonymized movie-watching data and determine, by evaluating reviews from users who had posted on the Internet Movie Database (IMDB), which users had watched which movies.[19] In recent months, Facebook has beefed up the control that users have over what information they share.

---

19 http://www.wired.com/politics/security/commentary/
    securitymatters/2007/12/securitymatters_1213

In the future, BDAs may emerge that let us decide not only which data to share, but also help us to understand the hidden implications of sharing personal information, whether that information identifies us personally or not.

Landscape Futures

Data and the algorithms designed to make use of it are becoming a fundamental and distinguishing asset for companies, both consumer- and business-focused.

File-sharing and collaboration solutions Box and Dropbox may well be considered BDAs given the huge volume of files they store. More and more BDAs are emerging that have a vertical focus. BDAs like oPower take the data from power meters and help consumers and businesses understand their power consumption and act on it to use energy more efficiently. Nest is a learning thermostat that understands consumer behavior and applies algorithms to the data it collects so that it can better heat and cool homes.

As more BDAs come to market, where does that leave infrastructure providers? When it comes to cloud-based infrastructure, it's likely that Amazon will have a highly competitive offering in virtually every area. And for those areas where it doesn't, the larger open-source infrastructure vendors may jump in to provide cloud-based offerings. If history is any indicator, it's probable that the big enterprise players, from EMC to IBM and Oracle, will continue to be extremely active acquirers of these vendors.

Going forward, expect more BDAs to emerge that allow consumers and businesses to put data to work. Some of those applications will help us better understand information—but many of them won't stop there. They'll go much further and automate the large number of activities that today we have to perform manually, whether that's publishing blog posts for optimal readership, or driving us to work.

Chapter Six

Big Data and the Next Billion-Dollar IPO

Billy Beane and Big Data

As general manager of the Oakland Athletics, Billy Beane faced a problem. Beane and the Oakland A's had to field a competitive team but do so without the big market budget of a team like the New York Yankees. In a story made famous by the movie *Moneyball* and the book of the same name by Michael Lewis, Beane turned to data and statistics.

This approach is known as sabermetrics, a term coined by baseball writer and statistician Bill James. Sabermetrics is a derivative of SABR, which stands for the Society for American Baseball Research. It is "the search for objective knowledge about baseball."[1]

At the time, Beane's data-driven approach was widely criticized. It broke with years of tradition of relying on the qualitative observations that scouts made about players. Instead it focused on using payroll to buy enough runs—not from a single player, but in aggregate—and thus, to buy wins.

---

1 http://seanlahman.com/baseball-archive/sabermetrics/sabermetric-manifesto/

Beane didn't use Big Data as it has traditionally been defined, as working with a volume of data bigger than the volume that traditional databases can handle. But he did apply data in a novel way.

Rather than making decisions purely based on qualitative information, Beane used a data-driven approach. More specifically, as Nate Silver points out in his best seller, *The Signal and the Noise: Why Most Predictions Fail but Some Don't*, Beane was disciplined about using the statistics that mattered—like on-base percentage—rather than those that didn't.[2]

Silver implemented the PECOTA system (short for Player Empirical Comparison and Optimization Test Algorithm) a sabermetric system widely used for forecasting the performance of Major League Baseball players. The PECOTA system draws on a database of some twenty thousand major league batters since World War II, as well as fifteen thousand minor league batters.[3]

Today, those who want to take a data-driven approach in their own organizations often face much the same challenge that Beane once faced. Taking a data-driven approach to decision making isn't easy. But as Billy Beane showed, it does produce results.

Organizations know they need to become more data-driven, but for them to do so, it has to be a lot easier for them to *be* data-driven. Big Data Applications (BDAs) are one of the key advances that make such an approach possible. That's one of the key reasons BDAs are poised to create tech's next billion-dollar IPOs.

---

2 http://bigdata.pervasive.com/Blog/Big-Data-Blog/EntryId/1123/It-s-Not-about-being-Data-Driven.aspx

3 http://en.wikipedia.org/wiki/PECOTA

Why Being Data-Driven Is Hard

Amazon, Google, IBM, and Oracle, to name a handful of the most valuable data-related companies on the planet, have shown the value of leveraging Big Data. Amazon serves billions of e-commerce transactions, Google handles billions of searches, and IBM and Oracle offer database software and applications designed for storing and working with huge amounts of data. Put simply, Big Data means big dollars.

Yet baseball isn't the only game in town that struggles to make decisions based on data. Most organizations still find making data-driven decisions difficult. In some cases, organizations simply don't have the data. Until recently, for example, it was hard to get comprehensive data on marketing activities. It was one thing to figure out how much you were spending on marketing, but it was another to correlate that marketing investment with actual sales. Thus the age-old marketing adage, "I know that half of my advertising budget is wasted, but I'm not sure which half."

Now, however, we're capturing data critical to understanding customers, supply chain, and machine performance—from network servers to cars to airplanes—and many other critical business indicators. The big challenge is no longer capturing the data; it's making sense of it.

For decades, making sense of data has been the province of data analysts, statisticians, and PhDs. Not only did a business line manager have to wait for IT to get access to key data, she then had to wait for an analyst to pull it all together and make sense of it. The promise of BDAs is the ability not just to capture data, but also to act on it, without requiring a set of tools that only statisticians can use. By making data more accessible, BDAs will enable organizations, one line of business at a time, to become more data-driven.

Yet even when we have the data and the tools to act on it, doing so remains difficult. Having an opinion is easy. Having conviction is hard.

As Warren Buffet once famously said, "Be fearful when others are greedy, and greedy when others are fearful."[4] Yet despite historical evidence that doing so is a bad idea, investors continue to invest on good news and sell on bad. Economists long assumed we made decisions based on logical rules, but in reality, we don't.[5]

Nobel Prize-winning psychologist Daniel Khaneman and his colleague Amos Tversky concluded that we often behave illogically. We give more weight to losses than to gains, and vivid examples often have a bigger impact on our decision-making than data, even if such data is more reliable.

To be data-driven, not only do we have to have the data and figure out which data is relevant, we then have to make decisions based on that data. To do that we have to have confidence and conviction—confidence in the data and the conviction to make decisions based on it—even when popular opinion tells us otherwise.

We refer to this as the Big Data Action Loop, and we'll explain the signal-noise component of it in the very next section.

---

4 http://www.nytimes.com/2008/10/17/opinion/17buffett.html?_r=0

5 http://www.nytimes.com/2002/11/05/health/a-conversation-with-daniel-kahneman-on-profit-loss-and-the-mysteries-of-the-mind.html

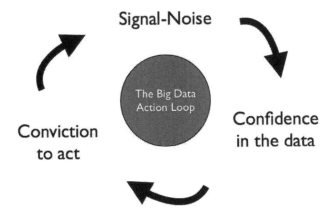

Put all this another way: It's one thing to agree with Warren Buffet. It's another to act like him.

The Signal And The Noise

That being data-driven is so hard, both culturally and from an implementation perspective is one of the key reasons that BDAs will play such an important role going forward. Historically, data was hard to get to and work with. Critically, data frequently wasn't in one place. Internal company data was spread across a variety of different databases, data stores, and file servers. External data was in market reports, on the web, and in other difficult-to-access sources.

The power, and the challenge, of Big Data is that Big Data often brings all that data together in one place. That means the potential for greater insights from larger quantities of more relevant data—what engineers call signal—but also for more noise, data that just isn't relevant to producing insights and can even result in drawing the wrong conclusions.

Just having the data in one place doesn't matter if computers or human beings can't make sense of the data. BDAs can help extract signal from noise. By doing so, they can give us more confidence in data, which will result in the conviction to act on that data, either manually or automatically.

The Big Data Feedback Loop

The first time you touched a hot stove, stuck your finger in an electrical outlet, or drove over the speed limit, you experienced a feedback loop. Consciously or not, you ran a test and analyzed the result. That result influenced your future actions. We call this the Big Data Feedback Loop and it is at the core of successful BDAs.

The Big Data Feedback Loop

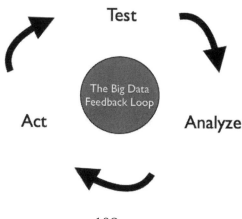

Test

Analyze

Act

The Big Data Feedback Loop

Through testing, you found out that touching a hot stove or getting an electrical shock hurt. You found out that speeding resulted in getting an expensive ticket or getting in a car crash. Or, if you got away with it, you may have concluded speeding was fun.

Regardless of the outcome, all of these activities gave you feedback. You incorporated this feedback into your personal data library and changed your future actions based on the data. If you had a fun experience speeding, you might have chosen to do more speeding. If you had a bad experience with a stove, you might have figured out to check if a stove was hot before touching one again.

Such feedback loops are critical when it comes to Big Data. Collecting data and analyzing it isn't enough. You have to be able to reach a set of conclusions from that data and get feedback on those conclusions to determine if they're right or wrong. The more relevant data you can feed into your model, and the more times you can get feedback on your hypotheses, the more valuable your insights are.

Historically, running such feedback loops has been slow and time consuming. We collected sales data, for example, and tried to draw conclusions about what pricing models or product features would cause people to buy more. We changed prices, revised features, and ran the experiment again. The problem is that by the time we concluded our analysis and revised our pricing and products, the environment had changed. Powerful but gas-guzzling cars were out, while fuel-saving cars were in. Myspace was out, while Facebook was in. And the list goes on.

The benefit of Big Data is that in many cases we can now run the feedback loop a lot faster. BDAs in advertising, for example, by serving up lots of different ads, can figure out which ones convert the best. They can even do this on a segmented basis—determining which ads convert the best for which groups of people. Humans could not do this kind of A/B testing, displaying different ads to see which perform better, fast enough to make the testing useful.

But computers can run such tests on a massive scale, not only choosing between different ads but actually modifying the ads themselves—different fonts, colors, sizes, or images—to figure out which are most effective. This real-time feedback loop, the ability not just to gather massive amounts of data but to test and act on many different approaches quickly, is one of the most powerful aspects of Big Data.

Minimum Data Scale

As we move forward with Big Data, it is becoming less a question of gathering and storing the data, and more a question of what to do with it. A high-performance feedback loop requires a sufficiently large test set—customers visiting websites, salespeople calling prospects, consumers viewing ads, and so on—to be effective.

We refer to this test set as Minimum Data Scale (MDS). MDS is the minimum amount of data required to run the Big Data Feedback Loop and get meaningful insights from it.

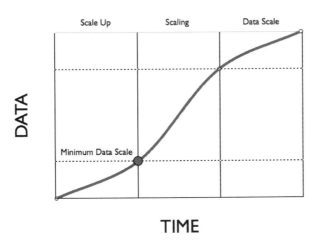

MDS means that a company has enough visitors to its website, viewers of its advertisements, or sales prospects, to allow it to derive meaningful conclusions and make decisions based on its tests. When a company has sufficient data to reach MDS, it can use Big Data Applications to tell salespeople whom to call next, decide which ad to serve for the highest conversion rate, or recommend the right movie or book.

When that data set becomes so large that it is a source of competitive advantage, it means a company has achieved what early PayPal and LinkedIn analytics guru Mike Greenfield refers to as Data Scale.[6] Companies like Amazon, Facebook, Google, PayPal, LinkedIn, and others have all achieved Data Scale.

---

6 http://numeratechoir.com/2012/05/

Big Data Applications

The power of BDAs is that they run part or all of the Big Data Feedback Loop. Some BDAs, powerful analytics and visualization applications for example, get the data in one place and make it viewable so that humans can decide what to do. Others test new approaches and decide what to do next automatically, as in the case of ad serving or website optimization.

The BDAs of today can't help significantly in reaching global maximums. They can't invent the iPhone or build the next Facebook. But they can fully optimize the local maximum. They can serve up the right ads, optimize web pages, tell salespeople whom to call, and even guide those salespeople in what to say during the call.

It is the combination of Data Scale and Applications—Big Data Applications—that will fuel tomorrow's billion-dollar IPOs.

The Rise Of The Big Data Asset

We refer to the large volume of data that companies collect as the Big Data Asset. Those that use it to their advantage will become more valuable than those that don't. They will be able to charge more and pay less, prioritize one prospect over another, convert more customers, and ultimately, retain more customers as well.

This has two major implications. First, when it comes to start-ups, there is a massive opportunity to build the applications that make such competitive advantage possible—as out-of-the-box solutions. Enterprises won't have to build these capabilities on their own; they'll get them as applications. Second, those companies (both start-ups and gorillas) that consider data and the ability to

112

act on it a core asset will have a significant competitive advantage over those that don't.

As an example, PayPal and Square are battling it out to disrupt the traditional payments ecosystem. The winner will understand its customers better and reach them more efficiently. Both companies have access to massive quantities of transaction data. The one that can act on it more effectively will come out on top.

What Does It Take To Build
A Billion-Dollar Company?

With all the opportunity in Big Data, what makes the difference between building a small company and building a big one?

As Cameron Myhrvold, managing partner at Ignition Partners, told me, building a billion-dollar company doesn't just mean picking a big market. It means picking the right market. Fast food in China is a huge market. But that doesn't make it a good market. It's highly competitive and a tough market to crack.

Building a billion-dollar company means riding a big wave. Big Data, cloud, mobile, and social are cliché for a reason—because they're big waves. Companies that ride those waves are more likely to succeed than those that don't. Of course, it's more than that. It's building specific products that align with those waves to deliver must-have value to customers.

Over the past few years, numerous web companies have sprung up. Some of the most successful ones, like Facebook and Twitter, are Big Data companies disguised as consumer companies. They store immense amounts of data. They have extensive digital versions of social

113

graphs that represent how we are connected to each other, and to other entities such as brands. Such companies have built-in systems for optimizing who sees what content, and who gets shown which ads.

Now there are multiple billion-dollar opportunities to bring these kinds of capabilities to enterprises, as out-of-the-box solutions in the form of Big Data Applications. For enterprises, historically, such data sophistication required buying hardware and software and layering custom applications on top of it.

Enterprise software products were the basis for such implementations. But they brought with them time-consuming integrations, expensive consulting, and custom development on top of core systems to make such sophistication available to users. Such custom development and the difficulty of moving off one major enterprise system and onto another that made it difficult for customers to switch from one vendor to another.

As an example, applications that would process the data necessary to notify a baggage-handling system when there was a flight delay were difficult and expensive to build. BDAs mean less custom development and more applications ready to address specific needs.

Beware The Bulk-Up

Given all the opportunity, perhaps the biggest challenge in reaching a billion for any startup able to get meaningful traction is the high likelihood of getting acquired first.

Historically, vendors and customers were both reliant on, and at odds with, each other. Customers wanted flexibility but couldn't switch due to their heavy custom development and integration investments, while vendors wanted to drive lock-in.

On the other hand, large customers needed comprehensive solutions. Even if one vendor didn't have the best technology in every area, choosing an integrated solution meant that the CIO or CEO of a big customer could call the CEO of a big vendor and get an answer or get an issue resolved.

In a time of crisis (system outage, data problems, or other issues) one C could call another C and make things happen. In a world of many complex and interconnected systems, flight scheduling, baggage routing, package delivery, and so on, that was—and remains—critical.

But when it comes to big vendors in the enterprise space, these days there are a lot of cooks in the kitchen. There are the traditional ultra-big companies, with market caps approaching or more than $100 billion: Cisco, IBM, Intel, Microsoft, Oracle, and SAP—with a mix of hardware and software offerings.

There are the ultra-big players that have an evolving or emerging role in the enterprise, like Amazon, Apple, and Google. There is the $20 to $50 billion group: HP, EMC, Salesforce, and VMWare.

Finally, there are those companies in the $10 billion and under range, like BMC, Informatica, NetApp, Workday, NetSuite, ServiceNow, Software AG, TIBCO, Splunk and others. This group is a mix of the new (like Workday, ServiceNow, and Splunk) and the older (like BMC and TIBCO). The smaller ones are potential takeover targets for the big. Cisco or IBM might be interested in Splunk, while Oracle or HP might want to buy TIBCO.

Existing public companies that can bulk up by adding more Big Data Applications to their portfolios will. Expect Salesforce and Oracle to keep on buying. Salesforce will continue to build out a big-enough and comprehensive-enough ecosystem that it can't easily be toppled. Oracle will add more cloud offerings, so that it can offer Big Data however customers want it—on-premise or in the cloud.

Companies like TIBCO and Software AG keep buying as well. Both companies have been building their cash war chests, likely with an eye toward building out their portfolios and adding non-organic revenue.

What does that mean for entrepreneurs trying to build the next billion-dollar public company? It means they need a great story, great revenue growth, or both. Splunk, for example, started out as a centralized way to view log files. It turned into the Oracle of machine data. That story certainly helped, but so did the company's growth.

The small will look to bulk up, and the big will look to stay relevant, ramp earnings, and leverage the immense scale of their enterprise sales organizations. That means that entrepreneurs with successful products and revenue growth, who want to surpass a billion dollars in market capitalization, will have to work hard not to get taken out too early.

Investment Trends

When it comes to Big Data, we are already seeing a host of new applications being built. The BDAs we've seen so far are just the tip of the iceberg. Many are focused on line-of-business issues. But many more will emerge to disrupt entire spaces and industries.

Take the police department of Santa Cruz, California, as an example. By analyzing historical arrest records, the police department is able to predict areas where crime will happen. The department can send police officers to areas where crime is likely to happen, which has been shown to reduce crime rates. That is, just having officers in the area at the right time of day or day of the week (based on a historical analysis), results in a reduction in crime. The police department of Santa Cruz is assisted by a company—PredPol—that works with this kind of Big Data to make it useful for that specific purpose.

The point is not that investors should back (or entrepreneurs should start) a hundred predictive-policing companies. Rather, it is that, as Myhrvold put it, Big Data is driving the creation of a whole new set of applications. It also means that Big Data isn't just for big companies. If the city of Santa Cruz is being shaped by Big Data, Big Data is going to affect companies of all sizes, as well as our own personal lives, from how we live and love, to how we learn. Big Data is no longer just for big companies that have large staffs of data analysts and engineers.

The infrastructure for analyzing Big Data is available, and (for entrepreneurs at least) much of that infrastructure is available in the cloud. It's easy to spin up and get started. Lots of public data sets are available to work with. As a result, entrepreneurs will create tons of BDAs. The challenge for entrepreneurs and investors will be to find interesting combinations of data, both public and private, and combine them in specific applications that deliver real value to lots of people over the next few years.

Data from review site Yelp, sentiment data from Twitter, government data about weather patterns—putting together these kinds of data sources could result in some very compelling applications. Banks might be able to better figure out whom to lend to, while a company picking its next store location might have better insight into where to locate it.

When it comes to big returns—at least in venture capital—it's about riding big waves. As Apple, Facebook, Google, and other big winners have shown, quite often it's not about being first. It's about having the best product that rides the wave.

The other waves investors are betting on are cloud, mobile, and social. Mobile, of course, is disrupting where, when, and how people consume media, interact, and do business. Cloud is making computing and storage resources readily available. And social is changing the way we communicate. Any one of these is a compelling wave to ride.

For entrepreneurs looking to build, and investors looking to back, the next billion-dollar opportunity, it really comes down to three things.

First, it is about choosing the right market, not just a big market. The best markets are ones that have the potential to grow rapidly. Second, it is about riding the wave: Big Data, cloud, mobile, or social. Third, as Gus Tai of Trinity Ventures put it, it is about being comfortable with a high level of ambiguity.

If the path is perfectly clear, then the opportunity is, by definition, too small. Clear paths are a lot more comfortable. We can see them. But opportunities that can be the source of a billion new dollars in value are inherently ambiguous. That requires entrepreneurs and investors who are willing to step out of their comfort zones. The next wave of billion-dollar Big Data entrepreneurs will be building BDAs where the path is ambiguous, but the goal is crystal clear.

Big Data 'Whitespace'

Big Data is opening up a number of new areas for entrepreneurship and investment. Products that make data more accessible, that allow analysis and insight development, without requiring one to be a statistician, engineer, or data analyst, are one major opportunity area. Just as Facebook has made it easier to share photos, new analytics products will make it easier not just to run analysis, but to share the results with others and learn from such collaboration as well.

The ability to pull together diverse internal data sources in one place, or to combine public and private data sources also opens up new opportunities for product creation and investment. New data combinations could lead to improved credit scoring, better urban planning, and the ability for companies to understand and act on market changes faster than their competition.

There will also be new information and data service businesses. Although lots of data is now on the web, from school performance metrics to weather information to US Census Data, lots of this data remains hard to access in its native form.

Zillow consolidated massive amounts of real-estate data and made it easy to access. The company went beyond for-sale listings, by compiling home-sales data that was stored in individual courthouses around the country. Services like Zillow will emerge in other categories. Gathering data, normalizing it, and presenting it in a fashion that makes it easily accessible is difficult. But the area of information services is ripe for disruption exactly because accessing such data is so hard.

New data services could also emerge as a result of new data that we generate. Since smartphones come with GPS, motion sensors, and built-in Internet connectivity, they are the perfection option for generating new location-specific data at a low cost.

Developers are already building applications to detect road abnormalities, such as potholes, based on vibration. That is just the first of a host of new BDAs based on collecting new data using low-cost sensors like smartphones.

Big Data Business Models

To get the optimal value from such white-space opportunities ultimately requires the financial markets to understand not just Big Data businesses, but subscription businesses as well.

Although Splunk is primarily sold via a traditional model, that is licensed software plus service, the company charges based on the amount of data indexed per day. As a result, investors can easily value Splunk on the volume of data that companies manage with it. Data volume is tied directly to revenue. (Splunk also offers a term license, wherein the company charges a yearly fee.)

For most cloud-based offerings, however, such valuations are not so simple. As Tien Tzuo, former chief marketing officer of Salesforce.com and CEO of cloud-based billing company Zuora, points out, financial managers still don't fully appreciate the value of subscription businesses.

This is important because companies will use subscription models to monetize many future BDAs. Tzuo suggests that such models are about building and monetizing recurring customer relationships. That's in contrast to their historical licensed-software and on-premise-hardware counterparts, which were "about building and shipping units for discrete, one-time transactions."[7] As Tzuo puts it, knowing that someone will give you a hundred dollars once

---

7 http://allthingsd.com/20121128/wall-street-loves-workday-but-doesnt-understand-subscription-businesses/

is a lot less valuable than knowing that that person will give you a hundred dollars a year for the next eight years.

In the years ahead, those companies that have subscription models will be well-positioned to hold onto their customers and maintain steady revenue streams. They won't have to rely on convincing existing customers to upgrade to new software versions in addition to the already hard job of acquiring new customers. Instead, they'll simply be able to focus on delivering value.

Apple effectively has the best of both in today's world: repeated one-time purchases in the form of iPads, iPhones, and Macs, combined with on-going revenue from the purchase of digital goods like songs and music. That said, even Apple, with its incredible brand-loyalty, may soon need to change its model to a recurring one. Companies like Spotify are making subscription-based music a viable alternative to one-time purchases.

Twenty years ago, it was hard for investors to imagine investing exclusively in software businesses. Now such investments are the norm. As a result, it's not hard to envision that despite today's skepticism, twenty years hence, most software businesses will be subscription businesses. At a minimum, their pricing will be aligned with actual usage in some way: more data, more cost; less data, less cost.

What such businesses will need to figure out, however, is how to offer predictability of pricing along with flexibility and agility. A number of different usage-based models exist, particularly for cloud offerings.

These include charging based on data volume; number of queries, as in the case of some analytics offerings; or on a subscription basis. Customers that take advantage of such offerings don't need to maintain their own hardware, power, and engineering-maintenance resources. More capacity is available when customers need it, less when they don't.

The cost of such flexibility, however, is less predictability. In most cases, such offerings should be less expensive than traditional software. Customers only pay for what they use.

It's easy to run over your mobile phone minutes and get an unexpectedly large bill. Similarly, customers can overuse—and overspend—on usage-based software offerings without realizing it.

Such ambiguity has slowed the adoption of some subscription-based services. Vendors will need to introduce better controls and built-in usage policies, so that buyers can more easily manage their spending. They'll need to make it easier not just to scale up, but to scale down as well, with little to no engineering effort.

Just over twenty years ago, limited partners who were considering putting capital into venture-capital funds thought that investing in software was a radical idea, says Mark Gorenberg, Managing Partner of Hummer Winblad Ventures. Previously such investors had put money primarily into hardware companies—for computer chips, networking equipment, and the like.

Limited partners of the time wondered if there would be any more companies like Microsoft. Now, of course, investing in telecom and hardware is out of favor, and software is the norm. For a long time, in business-to-business (B2B) software, that has meant investing in installed software. That's software that companies sell, and then charge for implementing, supporting, and upgrading. It requires vendors to fight an ongoing battle of convincing existing customers to upgrade to new versions just to maintain their existing revenue base.

Although vendors have much work to do in making subscription- and data-based pricing models easier to manage and budget, it is not hard to envision a world twenty years from now in which most pricing is subscription-based. That would mean that instead of financial managers discounting subscription-based companies, they would instead discount those companies that still sold on the traditional model of licensed software and service.

In such a future, those companies that had adjusted would be buying up and consolidating those that hadn't, instead of the reverse. If there is one truism of the tech industry, it is that while it takes the gorillas a long, long time to fall, without reinvention, fall they do. For cynics who claim that such things won't happen, just remember that we have short memories. One need look no further than at housing booms and busts.

As a result, there's always another billion-dollar company, and in the B2B space there is room for a few of them. With the waves of Big Data, cloud, mobile, and social setting the stage, it's not hard to imagine that the next twenty years of information technology will be even more exciting than the last twenty.

Chapter Seven

How Big Data Is Changing The Way We Live

The starting line at Ironman France 2012 was eerily quiet. There was a nervous tension in the air as twenty-five hundred people got ready to enter the water and spend as many as the next sixteen hours trying to complete what was for some the goal of a lifetime. Made famous by the Ironman World Championship held in Kona, Hawaii every year, an event that started out as a fifteen-person race in 1978 is now a global phenomenon.

Ironman contenders, like many athletes, are some of the most data-driven people on earth. To complete the race, which consists of a 2.4-mile swim and a 112-mile bike course, followed by a full 26.2-mile marathon, takes focus, perseverance, and training.

It also requires an incredible amount of energy. Ironman athletes burn some eight to ten thousand calories during the race.[1] To put that in perspective, human beings burn approximately two to two and a half thousand calories on an average day. Often called the fourth sport of triathlon, nutrition can mean the difference between finishing and bonking (athlete-speak for running out of energy).

---

1 http://www.livestrong.com/article/232980-the-calories-burned-during-the-ironman-triathlon/

As a result, both preparing for an Ironman and finishing the event itself requires incredible attention to data. Athletes who don't put in enough miles won't have enough endurance to finish come race day. And even those who have trained won't cross the finish line if they don't take in enough calories and water to keep their bodies moving.

In the fall of 2011, I decided to train for a full Ironman, and over the course of the next nine months, I learned more about training and nutrition and gathered more data about my personal fitness and health than I ever had before. I would regularly upload my training data to a website called Garmin Connect, developed by the well-known maker of GPS devices.

Remarkably, as of March 2013, athletes had logged nearly three billion miles on the Garmin Connect website. And they weren't just logging miles. When it comes to training and events, they were also logging elevation gain and loss, speed, revolutions per minute on their bikes, calories, and heart rate. Off the course, they were uploading metrics on their weight, body-fat percentage, body-water percentage, muscle mass, and daily calorie intake, among other health measurements.

One might think that capturing, storing, and analyzing such an immense amount of data would cost thousands, if not tens of thousands of dollars or more. But watches with built-in GPS are now available for under a hundred dollars, and scales that measure body composition cost around the same amount. Measurement devices come in all forms, and there are easy to use free and low-cost measurement and logging applications for iPhone and Android devices. What's more, the Garmin Connect service itself is free.

This combination of low-cost devices and applications for capturing a wide variety of data, combined with the ability to store and analyze large volumes of data at no cost, is an excellent example of the power of Big Data—not just for large enterprises but for all of us.

Personal Health Applications

Taking the capture and analysis of our personal health information one step further, by applying Big Data to personal genetics, is DNA-testing and data-analytics company 23andMe. Since its founding in 2006 by Anne Wojcicki, the company's CEO and wife of Google co-founder Sergey Brin, the company has analyzed the saliva of more than 180,000 people.

By analyzing our genomic data, the company identifies individual genetic disorders, such as Parkinson's, as well as genetic propensities such as obesity.[2] By amassing and analyzing a huge database of personal genetic information, the company hopes not only to identify individual genetic risk factors that may help people improve their health and live longer, but more general trends as well.

As a result of its analysis, the company has identified some 180 new traits, including one called the "photic sneeze reflex," which refers to the tendency to sneeze when moving from darkness to bright sunlight, and another associated with people's like or dislike of the herb cilantro.[3]

Using genomic data to provide insights for better healthcare is in reality the next logical step in an effort first begun in 1990. The Human Genome Project (HGP) had as its goal the mapping of all of the approximately 23,000 genes that were ultimately found to make

---

2 http://www.theverge.com/2012/12/12/3759198/23andme-genetics-testing-50-million-data-mining

3 https://www.23andme.com/health/photic-sneeze-reflex/

up our DNA. The project took thirteen years to complete and cost $3.8 billion.

Remarkably, storing human-genome data doesn't need to take up that much space. According to one analysis, human genes can be stored in as little as twenty megabytes, about the same amount of space as a handful of songs stored on an iPod.

How is that possible? About 99.5 percent of the DNA for any two randomly selected people is exactly the same.[4] Thus, by referring to a reference sequence of the human genome, it's possible to store just the information needed to turn the reference sequence into one that is specific to any one of us.

Although the DNA information of any individual takes up a lot of space in its originally sequenced form—a set of images of DNA fragments captured by high resolution camera—once those images are turned into the As, Cs, Gs, and Ts that make up our DNA, the sequence of any particular person can be stored in a highly efficient manner.

It is not always the ultimate size of the data that makes it Big Data. The ability not just to capture data, but also to analyze it in a cost-effective manner, is what really makes Big Data powerful. While the original sequencing of the human genome cost some $3.8 billion, today you can get an analysis of your own DNA for $99 from 23andMe. Industry experts believe that that price is subsidized, and that the actual cost of individual DNA analysis is more in the $500 to $1000 range. Even so, in just under a decade, the cost of sequencing has dropped by several orders of magnitude.

---

4 http://www.genetic-future.com/2008/06/how-much-data-is-human-genome-it.html

Of course, DNA sequencing alone isn't enough to improve our health. We must also make changes in our day to day lives.

Fitbit has the goal of making staying healthy easier by making it fun to do so. The company sells a small device that tracks your physical activity over the course of the day, as well as tracking your sleep patters at night. Fitbit also offers a free iPhone app that lets users log their food and liquid intake.

By tracking their activity levels and nutrition intake, users can figure out what's working well and what's not. Nutritionists advise that keeping an accurate record of what we eat and how much activity we engage in is one of the biggest factors in our ability to control our weight, because it makes us accountable.

Fitbit is collecting an enormous amount of information on people's health and personal habits. By doing so, it can show its users helpful charts to help them visualize their nutrition and activity levels, and make recommendations about areas for improvement.

Nike aims to accomplish something similar with the Nike+ FuelBand, a band that is worn around the wrist and gathers daily activity data. The device uses a built-in accelerometer to detect motion and track activities like running, walking, and even playing sports. Coupled with the Nike Plus website as well as mobile applications, the device makes it easier for users to track their activities, set goals, and change their habits.

Nike's offerings don't stop there. The company offers training programs for the well-known Xbox 360 gaming system that help users improve their fitness while at home. Such software enables users to virtually train with friends or other people in fitness communities. The idea is to make staying active fun and easy as well as social. People who train with a group benefit from increased motivation, higher accountability, and group camaraderie.[5]

Another device, the BodyMedia armband, captures over five thousand data points every minute, including information about temperature, sweat, steps, calories burned, and sleep quality.[6] The armband has been featured on NBC's *The Biggest Loser*, a reality game show focused on weight loss.

Strava combines real-world activity with virtual competition by taking such challenges outdoors. The company's running and cycling application for iPhone and Android devices is specifically designed to take advantage of the competitive nature of sporting activities. Fitness buffs can compete for leaderboard spots on a diverse set of real-world segments, such as cycling from the bottom to the top of a challenging hill, and compare their results on Strava's website. The company also offers pace, power, and heart rate analysis to help athletes improve.

According to an American Heart Association article entitled "The Price of Inactivity,"[7] 65 percent of all adults are obese or overweight. Sedentary jobs have increased 83 percent since 1950, and physically active jobs now make up only about 25 percent of the workforce. Americans work an average of forty-seven hours per week, 164 more hours per year than they did twenty years ago. In terms of costs, obesity costs American companies an estimated $225.8 billion per year in health-related productivity losses. As a result, devices like the Fitbit and the Nike FuelBand stand to make a real impact on rising healthcare costs and personal health.

---

5 http://www.active.com/fitness/Articles/3-Reasons-Its-Better-to-Work-Out-With-a-Group

6 http://www.bodymedia.com/Professionals/Health-Professionals

7 http://www.heart.org/HEARTORG/GettingHealthy/PhysicalActivity/StartWalking/The-Price-of-Inactivity_UCM_307974_Article.jsp

Another iPhone application can check your heart rate by reading your face or detecting the pulse rate in your finger. Biofeedback app-company Azumio has had more than twenty million downloads of its mobile applications, which can do everything from measuring your heart rate to detecting your stress level. Over time the company will be able to provide more and more compelling health insights as it measures data across an increasingly large population of users.

The company has already introduced a fitness application called Fitness Buddy that was featured in *ESPN Magazine*, and Sleepy Time, an application for monitoring sleep cycles using an iPhone. Such applications present intriguing possibilities for Big Data and health.

Data collected by such applications can tell us what's going on in the moment, as well as offer us a picture of our health over time. For example, if our resting heart rate is fluctuating, that may indicate a change in our health status. By working with health data collected across millions of people, scientists can develop better algorithms for predicting future health. Applications can give us better suggestions about what changes we should make to improve our health.

Historically, monitoring health information over time required specialized devices, or an inconvenient and expensive trip to the doctor's office. One of the most compelling aspects of new applications is the way in which they make it easier to monitor such health information.

The availability of low-cost personal health monitoring applications and related technologies has even spawned an entire movement in personal health. Quantified Self is "a collaboration of users and tool makers who share an interest in self-knowledge through self-tracking."[8] The founders of the Quantified Self movement are two former editors of *Wired* magazine, Kevin Kelly and Gary Wolf. Wolf is known for both his TED talk,[9] "The quantified self," in which he highlights all of the data we can collect about ourselves, and his 2010 *New York Times* article, "The Data Driven Life."[10]

New applications show just how much heath data can be collected with inexpensive devices, or devices like smartphones that we already have, when combined with the right software applications. Put that data-collection ability together with low-cost cloud services for analysis and visualization, and the area of personal health and Big Data has significant potential to improve health and reduce healthcare costs.

Big Data And The Doctor

Despite such applications, there are times when we need to go to the doctor. A lot of medical information is still collected with pen and paper. Pen and paper have the benefit of being easy to use and low-cost. But such an approach also results in errors when it comes to patient care and billing. Having paper-based records spread across multiple locations can make it difficult for healthcare providers to access critical information about a patient's health history.

The HITECH Act (Health Information Technology for Economic and Clinical Health) was enacted in 2009 to promote the use of health information technology, and in particular, the adoption of Electronic Health Records, or EHRs. It offers healthcare providers

---

8 http://quantifiedself.com/about/

9 http://www.ted.com/talks/gary_wolf_the_quantified_self.html

10 http://www.vanityfair.com/culture/2013/02/quantified-self-hive-mind-weight-watchers and http://www.nytimes.com/2010/05/02/magazine/02self-measurement-t.html

financial incentives to adopt EHRs through 2015, and imposes penalties on those who don't adopt EHRs after that time. Electronic Medical Records (EMRs) are digital versions of the paper records that many physicians use today. In contrast, an EHR is intended as a common record of a patient's health that can be easily accessed by multiple healthcare providers.[11]

New applications like drchrono allow physicians to capture patient information using iPads, iPhones, Android devices, or a web browser. In addition to capturing the kind of patient information previously recorded using pencil and paper, doctors get integrated speech-to-text for dictation, the ability to capture photos and videos, and other functionality.

Electronic Health Records, DNA testing, and newer imaging technologies are generating huge amounts of data. Capturing and storing such data presents a challenge for healthcare providers but also an opportunity. In contrast to historically closed hospital IT systems, newer, more open systems, combined with digitized patient information, could provide insights that lead to medical breakthroughs.

In fact, IBM's Watson computer—the same computer famous for winning *Jeopardy!*—is now being used by the Memorial Sloan-Kettering Cancer Center to develop better decision-support systems for cancer treatment.[12] The hope is that by analyzing data from EHRs and academic research Watson will be able to provide doctors with better information for making decisions about cancer treatments.

---

11 http://www.healthit.gov/buzz-blog/electronic-health-and-medical-records/emr-vs-ehr-difference/

12 http://healthstartup.eu/2012/05/top-big-data-opportunities-for-health-startups/

Such analysis can lead to additional insights as well. For example, an intelligent system can alert a doctor to other treatments and procedures normally associated with the one he's recommending. Such systems can also provide busy doctors with more current information on the latest research in a particular area.

The amount of data that all these systems capture and store is staggering. More and more patient data will be stored digitally, and not just the kind of information that we provide on health questionnaires, or that doctors record on charts. Such information also includes digital images from devices like iPhones and iPads, and from newer medical imaging systems, such as x-ray machines and ultrasound devices, which now produce digital images.

In terms of Big Data, that means better and more efficient patient care in the future, the ability to do more self-monitoring and preventative health maintenance, and, of course, a lot more data to work with. The challenge will be to make sure that data isn't just collected for the sake of collecting it, but that it can be used to provide key insights to both healthcare providers and individuals. Making the capture and viewing of data easier is a small, but critical step in the path toward reaping the benefits of Big Data applied to health.

Why We Still Can't Cure Cancer

In December of 2011, I got a rather strange e-mail from my dad. Holding a doctorate in chemistry, my dad thrived on data. He had had some tests done that showed that his PSA levels were significantly above normal. PSA, I would later find out, stands for Prostate-Specific Antigen.

Higher PSA levels are highly correlated with prostate cancer. This raised two key questions. The first was whether my dad actually had cancer. The test did not reveal cancer cells. Rather, higher levels of PSA are often found in people who ultimately are diagnosed with prostate cancer. The difficulty is that not all people with higher PSA levels have cancer. Some of them just have higher PSA levels.

The second challenge my dad faced was what to do with the information. His options were at the same time simple and complex. On the one hand, he could do nothing. As one doctor I spoke with told me, "It's usually something else that kills them." However, my dad would have to live with the psychological impact of having a slowly worsening disease, which ultimately might spread at a time when he could be too old to do anything about it.

On the other hand, he could take action. Action would come in the form of a range of treatments, from hormone therapy to ablative surgery to the complete removal of his prostate. But the treatment might prove worse than the cure.

"What should I do?" my dad asked the doctor. The doctor gave him the only answer he could: "It's up to you. It's your life."

In the course of hormone therapy, which is the route he ultimately chose, my dad suffered depression, cold sweats, and experienced extensive periods of difficulty sleeping. A few months later, a research study was published indicating that the best treatment for prostate cancer may to be not to test for it at all. Apparently, the microscopic hole associated with the tests can allow the cancer, which is contained in the prostate gland, to escape.

Therein lie two important lessons about our use of data.

First, data can give us greater insights. It can deliver more relevant experiences and allow computers to predict what movie we'll want to watch, or what book we'll want to buy next. But when it comes to things like medical treatment, the decisions about what to do with those insights aren't always obvious.

Second, our insights from data can evolve. Insights from data are based on the best data we have available at the time. Just as fraud-detection systems try to identify fraudsters based on pattern recognition, those systems can be improved with better algorithms based on more data. Similarly, the suggested approaches to different medical conditions change as we get more data.

In men, the leading causes of cancer death are lung, prostate, liver, and colorectal cancer, while in women the leading causes are lung, breast, and colorectal cancer. Smoking, a leading cause of lung cancer, has dropped from a rate of 45 percent of the US population in 1946 to 25 percent in 1993 to 19.3 percent as of 2010.[13] However, the five-year survival rate for those with lung cancer is only 15.5 percent, a figure that hasn't changed in forty years.[14]

Despite then-president Richard Nixon declaring a national war on cancer in 1971, there remains no universal prevention or cure for cancer. That's in large part because cancer is really hundreds of diseases, not just one: there are more than two hundred different types of cancer.[15]

The National Cancer Institute (NCI), which is part of the National Institutes of Health, has a budget of about $5 billion per year for cancer research.[16] Some of the biggest advances in cancer research

---

13 http://www.cdc.gov/tobacco/data_statistics/fact_sheets/fast_facts/

14 http://www.lungcancerfoundation.org/who-we-are/the-right-woman-for-the-job/

15 http://www.cancerresearchuk.org/cancer-help/about-cancer/cancer-questions/how-many-different-types-of-cancer-are-there

16 http://obf.cancer.gov/financial/factbook.htm

have been the development of tests to detect certain types of cancer, such as a simple blood test discovered in 2004 to predict colon cancer.

Other advances have been those that link cancer to certain causes, such as a study in 1954 that first showed a link between smoking and lung cancer, and a study in 1955 that showed that the male hormone testosterone drives the growth of prostate cancer, while the female hormone estrogen drives the growth of breast cancer. Still further advances have come in the approaches to treating cancer: the discovery, for example, of dendritic cells, which became the basis for cancer vaccines, and the discovery of angiogenesis, the process by which tumors create a network of blood vessels to bring them the oxygen that allows them to grow.[17]

More recently, Big Data has been playing a bigger role. The National Cancer Institute's CellMiner, for example, is a web-based tool that gives researchers access to large quantities of genomic-expression and chemical-compound data. Such technology makes cancer research more efficient. In the past, working with such datasets often meant dealing with unwieldy databases that made it difficult to analyze and integrate data.[18]

Historically, there was a big gap between the people who wanted to answer questions by using such data and those who had access to the data. Technologies like CellMiner make that gap smaller. Researchers used CellMiner's predecessor, a program called COMPARE, to identify a drug with anticancer activity, which turned out to be helpful in treating some cases of lymphoma. Those researchers are now using CellMiner to figure out biomarkers that

---

17 http://www.webmd.com/prostate-cancer/features/fifty-years-of-milestones-in-cancer-research

18 http://www.cancer.gov/ncicancerbulletin/100212/page7

will tell them which patients are likely to respond favorably to the treatment.

One of the biggest impacts the researchers cite is the ability to access data more easily. That is a critical lesson not just for cancer researchers but for anyone hoping to take advantage of Big Data—unless the large amounts of data collected are made readily accessible, they'll remain limited in their use. Democratizing Big Data—opening up access to it—is critical.

Other Illnesses

According to the Centers for Disease Control (CDC), heart disease is the leading cause of death in the United States, accounting for almost six hundred thousands deaths each year, out of a total of nearly 2.5 million deaths.[19] Cancer accounts for just slightly fewer deaths. AIDS is the sixth leading cause of death among people aged twenty-five to forty-four in the United States, down from the number one cause in 1995.[20] About two-thirds of all deaths in the US each year are due to natural causes.

What about that much less serious, but far-reaching illness, the common cold? It's estimated that people in the US catch a billion colds each year. That's three colds for every person. The common cold is caused by rhinoviruses, some ninety- nine of which have been sequenced,[21] and the number of different strains has historically been the reason the common cold is so hard to cure.

---

19 http://www.cdc.gov/nchs/fastats/deaths.htm
20 http://www.ncbi.nlm.nih.gov/pubmedhealth/PMH0001620/
21 http://www.ncbi.nlm.nih.gov/pubmed/19213880

Although there's no cure on the immediate horizon, scientists have found commonalities in the proteins that make up the different forms of the virus, which may lead to advances in the future.

There are more than seven billion people living on the planet, according to estimates by the US Census Bureau and the United Nations Population Fund.[22] Big Data applied to healthcare isn't just about addressing non-natural causes of death. It's also about increasing access to healthcare, improving quality of life, and reducing the costs associated with lost time and productivity due to poor health.

In 2011, the United States spent about $2.7 trillion on healthcare, or about $8,650 per person. As people continue to live longer and fewer children die, more people are grappling with chronic illnesses and diseases that strike later in life.[23] More children are receiving vaccines that are reducing the deaths of children under the age of five, while outside of Africa, obesity has become a greater problem than malnutrition. In research that the Bill & Melinda Gates Foundation funded along with others, scientists found that people around the world are living longer, but they're also sicker. All of this points to the need for more efficiency in delivering healthcare and in helping people track and improve their own health as much as possible.

Big Data And Where We Live

Big Data isn't just improving health and well-being by changing the way we live, it's also changing the environments in which we

---

22 http://en.wikipedia.org/wiki/World_population

23 http://www.salon.com/2012/12/13/study_people_worldwide_living_longer_but_sicker/

live. Smart cities hold the promise of helping cities better organize for growth, according to the World Bank.[24] The promise of smart cities "is their ability to collect, analyze, and channel data in order to make better decisions at the municipal level through the greater use of technology." When it comes to "urban data, we are today where we were in the 1930s on country or national level data," according to Christopher Williams of UN Habitat.

Today, more than half of the world's population lives in urban areas, and that number is expected to rise to three-quarters of the population by 2050. One challenge in collecting data from cities is standardizing the kinds of data that are collected. Cities use a diverse set of data collection methods and collect different kinds of data, making it difficult to compare data from multiple cities to develop best practices. But cities that are able to gather relevant data can make better decisions about infrastructure investments. That's important given how long such investments tend to last.[25]

Devices like smart energy meters are already measuring energy consumption and providing consumers with detailed reports on their energy usage. In cities like San Francisco, smart parking meters are reporting the availability of parking on city streets, data that is then accessible to drivers via easy-to-use mobile apps. Those same parking meters work with products from PayByPhone, to enable people to pay for parking by calling a phone number or using a mobile application. Some three million people now make use of the company's offering in 180 cities, including London, Miami, Vancouver, and San Francisco.

---

24 http://web.worldbank.org/WBSITE/EXTERNAL/TOPICS/EXTSDNET/0,,co
    ntentMDK:23146568~menuPK:64885113~pagePK:7278667~piPK:64911
    824~theSitePK:5929282,00.html

25 http://mercuryadvisorygroup.com/articles/sustain/100-pt4-reischl.html

Meanwhile, applications are making it easier to get around major cities. CabSense analyzes data from the New York City Taxi & Limousine Commission and other sources to tell users the best corner on which to catch a cab based on the day of the week, the time of the day, and their location. CabSense has analyzed tens of millions of historical data points and uses the data to rate every street corner on a scale of one to five.

Other apps tell users the best ways to make use of public transportation, and even the best train car to be in to make the fastest exit from the subway. Through a combination of applications that cities provide, or at least sponsor the development of, and private application developers' innovative uses of publicly available data, cities are becoming easier to navigate, and municipal governments are getting more information about what services will be most helpful to city residents. Mobile devices may be one of the easiest ways for smart cities to collect the critical data that enables them to improve services and make better decisions about infrastructure investments.

The Mobile Future

Nearly five decades after the concept was introduced on Star Trek in 1966, the possibility of a handheld medical tricorder is becoming a reality.[26] Smartphone applications can now measure our heart rates and stress levels. Low-cost smartphone add-ons can gauge glucose levels and even provide ultrasound at home.

Such consumer applications and devices hold the promise of making some aspects of healthcare, at least health monitoring,

---

26 http://www.economist.com/news/technology-quarterly/21567208-medical-technology-hand-held-diagnostic-devices-seen-star-trek-are-inspiring

more widely available and cost-effective. The data that such devices generate not only provides information useful to patients, but also to doctors performing diagnosis, and to scientists who rely on large quantities of data to inform their research. Smartphones combined with low-cost medical add-ons may be one of the lowest cost and most efficient ways to expand access to health technology.

Some estimates put the number of smartphones in use worldwide at more than a billion, and the addition of the next billion devices could come as soon as 2015.[27] Mobile phone connectivity is on the rise in sub-Saharan Africa, reaching a penetration rate of more than 62 percent as of 2011, and smartphones, according to one writer, are not far behind.[28] Such devices come with built-in connectivity, making it easy for them to report data and receive updates.

As in other areas of Big Data, it is at the intersection of the growing number of relatively inexpensive sensors for collecting data—such as iPhones and the specialized medical add-ons for them—and the amount of data those sensors generate, where some of the most promising advances lie in improving healthcare and access to it. Combined with the digitization of medical records and more intelligent systems that can give doctors better information, Big Data promises to have a big impact on our health, both at home and in the doctor's office.

---

27 http://thenextweb.com/mobile/2012/10/17/global-smartphone-users-pass-1-billion-for-the-first-time-report/

28 http://techcrunch.com/2012/06/09/feature-phones-are-not-the-future/

Chapter Eight

Big Data Meets Romance

Big Data And Online Dating

Online dating website OkCupid, which was acquired by Match.com in 2011, conducted a series of research studies on what makes for the most successful online dating profiles. In a post entitled "The 4 Big Myths of Profile Pictures," OkCupid researchers described the results of analyzing more than seven thousand profile photos to figure out which ones produced the best results, as measured by the number of messages each user received.[1]

Of course, just receiving more messages isn't necessarily a good thing. Quality is often more important than quantity. But before we explore that issue, let's first take a look at what the researchers found.

The researchers characterized photos into one of three categories: flirty-face, smiling, and not smiling. Flirty-face refers to "flirting directly into the camera," as opposed to smiling or just looking happy.

The researchers discovered that for women, eye contact in online profile pictures was critical. Those with a flirty-face got slightly

---

1 http://blog.okcupid.com/index.php/the-4-big-myths-of-profile-pictures/

more messages each month than those without and significantly more messages than those who were characterized as not smiling.

Without eye contact, the results were significantly worse. Regardless of facial expression, those who didn't make eye contact with the camera (and therefore with the viewer of the photo) received fewer messages overall than those who did.

In contrast to women, men had the most success in meeting women when they used profile pictures in which they were looking away from the camera and not smiling. Men who used photos that showed them flirting and looking away from the camera had the least success in meeting women. The researchers also found that for men, wearing "normal clothes" in a photo or being "all dressed up" did not make much of a difference when it comes to meeting a potential mate.

In perhaps one of their most interesting findings, the researchers discovered that whether or not you show your face in a photo doesn't have a big impact on how many messages you receive. Photos of people in scuba gear, walking across the dessert, or with their faces out of the camera completely were about as likely to help users of the site generate interest as those photos in which users showed their faces.

Women who used photos showing their faces received, on average, 8.69 contacts per month, while those who didn't show their faces received 8.66 messages per month. Men who used facial photos met 5.91 women for every ten attempts, while those not showing their faces met 5.92 women for every ten attempts.

The researchers' conclusion? The photos do all the work. They "pique the viewer's curiosity and say a lot about who the subject is (or wants to be)." It's important to note, as the authors of the study stated, "We wouldn't recommend that you meet someone in person without first seeing a full photo of them."

What all that means is that Big Data isn't just a tool for business—given the right data sources, it can also give us insights into how best to portray ourselves to find the right mate. The other takeaway, of course, is that you shouldn't underestimate the importance of choosing the right photo, based on the data.

Lies, Damn Lies, And Statistics

Of course, people are known to stretch the truth when it comes to online dating. In another study, OkCupid co-founder Christian Rudder looked at data from some 1.51 million active users of the dating site.

In "The Big Lies People Tell In Online Dating,"[2] Rudder reported his discovery that when it comes to height, "almost universally, guys like to add a couple inches." In fact, as guys "get closer to six feet," they round up more than usual, "stretching for that coveted psychological benchmark." Women also exaggerate their height, "though without the lurch towards a benchmark height."

What about income? Do people who claim to make $100,000 a year or more, really make that much? When it comes to online dating, Rudder found that people are 20 percent poorer than they say they are. As we get older, we tend to exaggerate more, with people in their forties and fifties exaggerating by 30 percent or more. People don't just alter their income; they also upload photos that are out of date. Rudder's research found that "the more attractive the picture, the more likely it is to be out of date."

---

2 http://blog.okcupid.com/index.php/the-biggest-lies-in-online-dating/

So how do the dating sites decide what potential matches to show you?

Match.com, which has some 1.8 million paying subscribers, introduced a set of new algorithms, code-named Synapse, to analyze "a variety of factors to suggest possible mates," according to an *FT.com* article, "Inside Match.com."[3]

What we say we're looking for isn't always what we're actually looking for. Although the algorithm takes into account people's stated preferences, it also factors in the kind of profiles that users actually look at. For example, if a user states a preference for a certain age range but looks at potential mates outside that range, the algorithm takes that into account and includes people outside the range in future search results.

What makes the challenge of predicting preferences even more complicated is that unlike with movie or book recommendations, algorithms that match human beings together have to take into account mutual preferences. "'Even if you like *The Godfather, The Godfather* doesn't have to like you back,'" Amarnath Thombre, head of analytics at Match.com, was quoted as saying.

The challenge with such algorithms is that although Match.com has data on the seventy-five million users who have registered on the site since its founding in 1995, it doesn't have data on which dates are successful, and which ones aren't. This inability to close the loop is an important missing element in creating the ultimate matchmaking algorithm.

---

3 http://www.ft.com/intl/cms/s/2/f31cae04-b8ca-11e0-8206-00144feabdc0.
   html

That's why when people cancel their subscriptions, dating sites often ask whether the reason is because they're dissatisfied with their online dating experience or because they met someone. Not only is such data useful for marketing, it can also, in theory, factor into predictive algorithms as well.

The Missing Data

But it is just that kind of missing data that may be causing machine-matching algorithms to fail. As with all Big Data analytics and predictive engines, such algorithms are only as good as the data that engineers used to develop them, and the data they're fed. If key data is missing, predictive algorithms won't work.

Eli J. Finkel from Northwestern University and Benjamin R. Karney at the University of California, Los Angeles, the authors of a study published in the journal *Psychological Science in the Public Interest* point out in their study and in a corresponding *New York Times* opinion piece that what really matters is how people interact when they meet each other in person, not what they say online.[4]

"Things like communication patterns, problem-solving tendencies, and sexual compatibility are crucial for predicting the success or failure of relationships," say the two professors.

They also point out that the way in which "couples discuss and attempt to resolve disagreements predicts their future satisfaction and whether or not the relationship is likely to dissolve." These, however, are not the sorts of characteristics that are easily evaluated in the context of an online dating site. Moreover, dating sites

---

4 http://www.nytimes.com/2012/02/12/opinion/sunday/online-dating-sites-dont-match-hype.html

don't factor in the environment of a relationship, stresses such as "job loss, financial strain, infertility, and illness."

The authors also point out that while dating sites may collect a lot of information, such information is a very small piece of the pie when it comes to figuring out what will make two people a good long-term match. While many sites claim to match people based on common interests, a 2008 study of 313 other studies found that "similarity of personality traits and attitude had no effect on relationship well-being in established relationships."

A 2010 study of more than twenty-three thousand married couples showed that having major personality attributes in common, such as neuroticism, impulsivity, and extroversion only accounted for half a percent of marital satisfaction, meaning that 99.5 percent was due to other factors.

The conclusion of the studies' authors? Online dating isn't any better or worse than any other way to meet potential mates. While the algorithms online dating sites use may make for good marketing, such algorithms may ultimately just be a way to help users of such sites get started with their online dating experience, and to provide a manageable pool of potential mates in densely populated areas such as New York City.

What such research really points out from a Big Data perspective is the importance of having complete data. Whether algorithms are trying to recommend movies, tell salespeople which customers to call next, or suggest potential mates, the algorithms are only as good as the data. Without sufficient data and a way to close the loop (by knowing whether an algorithm made a correct prediction or not), it's difficult to create accurate algorithms. Like throwing darts at a dartboard, getting all the darts in the same area doesn't matter if that area isn't the bull's-eye.

Predicting Marriage Success

When it comes to prediction, one scientist is able to predict with astounding accuracy which matches are likely to succeed. Professor of psychology Dr. John Gottman is famous for running a physiology lab, known as the "Love Lab," at the University of Washington.

Gottman has studied more than 650 couples over a period of fourteen years. Based on his research, Gottman can predict with over 90-percent accuracy based on a half-hour interview with a recently married couple whether their marriage will last.[5]

Gottman refers to what he calls mental map-making as the basis for romance. Mental map-making, in the context of a relationship, is the process of finding out about our partners. One simple example of mental map-making Gottman provides is of men who have an interest in what their wives are going to do on a given day.

An active mental-map maker not only gathers information but also thinks about that information during the day and follows up on it later. That means asking about a spouse's meeting, lunch, or an event the couple discussed over breakfast.

It might seem obvious, but the process of gathering data, thinking about that data, and following up on that data is not only useful in computing, but in maintaining a healthy relationship as well.

Gottman and his colleague, Professor James Murray, took things even further and developed mathematical models of biological research. They created mathematical models of human behavior that they used to analyze and predict marriage success. The two profes-

---

5 http://www.uwtv.org/video/player.aspx?pid=OJG2Xv9kB9n0

sors, along with several others, even published a book entitled *The Mathematics of Marriage: Dynamic Nonlinear Models.*

Gottman and his fellow authors believe that "the development of marriage is governed—or at least can be described—by a differential equation."[6] Gottman and his colleagues are able to describe a marriage using the mathematics of calculus and simulate how a couple will act under various conditions.

Gottman's research discovered four negative behaviors that frequently predict divorce: criticism of a partner's personality, contempt, defensiveness, and emotional withdrawal from interaction.[7] Gottman describes contempt, in particular, as "sulfuric acid for love."

By combining an evaluation of a couple's responses to various questions, analysis of body language, and biological data, with mathematical models, Gottman can not only predict whether a marriage is on course to succeed, but can also suggest immediate changes for course correction if it isn't.

Given all this talk of mathematics and differential equations, it might seem like Gottman is taking the magic out of romance, but as Gottman puts it, it's important for scientists and researchers to have an objective model for measuring human relationships.

In a video interview, Gottman revealed some other interesting data points. Couples who didn't have a baby in the first seven years of marriage had a 50 percent divorce rate, while couples who did have a baby had only a 25 percent divorce rate. However, of those who stayed married, 75 percent suffered from a downward trend

---

6 http://www.slate.com/articles/life/do_the_math/2003/04/love_by_the_numbers.2.html

7 http://en.wikipedia.org/wiki/John_Gottman and http://psycnet.apa.org/?&fa=main.doiLanding&doi=10.1037/0893-3200.14.1.42

in marital happiness; in other words, they became unhappier with their marriages over time.

There is a silver lining to this seemingly depressing news, however. Gottman studied the 25 percent who remained happy with their marriages to figure out what kept their relationships happy. His conclusions were that couples who focused on preserving knowledge of each other, mutual admiration, and affection for each other were more likely to end up in the 25 percent group, rather than the 75 percent. In particular, to keep a marriage in the 25 percent bucket, couples had to be five times as positive with each other as negative.

Can marriages be saved? Many couples who go through marriage counseling relapse after two years, falling into the same old habits. However, based on two studies, Gottman concluded that there are two active ingredients that can produce lasting positive effect on a marriage: first, reducing negativity in conflict resolution; second, increasing overall positivity by focusing on helping partners in a marriage "be better friends."

How Facebook Is Shaping Relationships

While Gottman and his colleagues are helping couples in the offline world based on their years of research, perhaps no online company is having a bigger impact on relationships than social networking giant Facebook.

The company, which now has more than a billion users worldwide, is the go-to destination for photo sharing, status updates, and a timeline of your life—both on your own and with others.

Social networking sites like Facebook represent such relationships in something called the social graph. Unlike the single connective line of a one-to-one relationship, a social graph consists of many interconnected relationships. If Joe knows Fred, and Fred knows Sarah, then in the context of the social graph, Joe has a link to Sarah through Fred. But such interconnections extend even further with the inclusion of interests, places, companies, brands, birthdays, and status updates, among other non-human elements. In the context of the social graph, people have connections not just with other people, but with activities, events, companies, and products.

The concept of six degrees of separation has popularized the notion that any two people are at most six steps away from each other in terms of social connections. Business networking site LinkedIn takes advantage of this concept by showing businesspeople how they're connected to other people through intermediary relationships. These professionals then take advantage of this connectivity when they want to talk with people they don't know directly, but who are a friends of a friend, or colleagues of a colleague.

At Facebook, people are even closer to each other than the six degrees concept might suggest. Sanjeev Kumar, an engineering manager at the company, indicated that Facebook users are highly connected, with an average 4.74 degree of separation between any two Facebookers.[8] Relationships in the social graph are made denser due to connections with places, interests, and other elements.

By representing the relationships between a very large number of connections, the social graph can answer lots of interesting Big Data questions. That includes not only questions posed by data analysts, but questions actively or passively posed by hundreds of millions of users, such as: with whom should I connect? What photos should I look at? Which information is important to me?

---

8 http://www.ece.lsu.edu/hpca-18/files/HPCA2012_Facebook_Keynote.pdf

Although most of these users don't think of themselves as performing queries against the Big Data that is the social graph, that is exactly what they're doing—or at least what social networking services are doing on their behalf.

Social graphs are equally interesting in Big Data from a technical perspective. Answering questions such as the ones above consumes a lot of computing resources. Each query involves working with a very large subset of the overall graph (known in technical terms as the working set) and is highly customized to each user.

What's more, the social graph represents lots of actual data—not just the interconnections in the graph itself, but the photos, videos, status updates, birthdays, and other information associated with each user. A query has to return the right set of relationships. It also has to return the data associated with those relationships and do so nearly instantaneously.

The social graph represents so much data that to keep up with it, Facebook has had to develop custom servers, build out its own data centers, and design special software for querying the graph, and for efficiently storing and retrieving its associated data.

So what does all this mean for our relationships?

Relationship Status

Of the many ways to express ourselves on Facebook, "relationship status is the only one that directly involves another person."[9] We commonly announce engagements, marriages, breakups, and divorces on the social-networking site.

---

9 http://www.time.com/time/business/article/0,8599,1895694,00.html

In 2010, about 60 percent of Facebook users set a relationship status on their profile, and as of December of that year, women outnumbered men by a rate of 1.28 to 1.[10] In 2011, a third of all divorce filings mentioned the word Facebook, up from 20 percent the previous year.[11]

Announcing our relationship status online can strengthen what researchers refer to as "feeling rule reminders."[12] Such rules are the social norms that tell us when and what to feel, and how strong our emotions should be. By declaring our relationship status online, we reinforce such rules.

Social networking sites like Facebook can also affect one's health and personality. Some people present themselves authentically on the site, while others present themselves in an improved light due to feelings of insecurity.[13]

About 24 percent of Americans and 28 percent of Brits have admitted to lying or exaggerating on a social network about what they've done or whom they've met, according to statistics cited by Cara Pring of social networking-statistics site *The Social Skinny*.[14] Moreover, visiting our profiles too frequently can make us overly aware of ourselves, causing stress and anxiety.

At the same time, having more digital friends than others—the average Facebook user has 229 friends on the social network—may

---

10 http://blogs.channel4.com/benjamin-cohen-on-technology/the-way-facebook-changes-relationships/2541

11 http://abcnews.go.com/Technology/facebook-relationship-status/story?id=16406245#.UMzUJaWTVjY

12 http://doctorat.sas.unibuc.ro/wp-content/uploads/2010/11/Issue2_GregBowe_Romantic.pdf

13 http://allfacebook.com/infographic-facebook-hurt-relationships_b45018

14 http://thesocialskinny.com/216-social-media-and-internet-statistics-september-2012/

give us a shot of self-confidence due to receiving additional social support. Some 25 percent of people believe that social networks have boosted their confidence. Having fewer friends than others may make us feel self-conscious, but the smaller digital circle may also lead to more genuine interactions.

In case there is any doubt about how big an impact online socializing is having on our lives, 40 percent of people spend more time socializing online than they do having face-to-face interactions. Internet users spend 22.5 percent of their online time engaged in social networking activities, with more than half of all Facebook users returning to the site on a daily basis.

Social Capital

We value our online identities, and the relationships they enable, not just because they are a way to express ourselves, but also because we associate them with social capital. Social capital is the benefit we receive from our position in a social network and the associated connections and resources that are a part of that network, both online and offline.

Such capital comes in two forms, *bonding* and *bridging*, according to researchers at the Human-Computer Interaction Institute at Carnegie Mellon University and at Facebook.[15] Bonding refers to social capital derived from relationships with family members and close friends, while bridging refers to that derived from acquaintances.

Both have value, but bonding typically enables emotional support and companionship. Bridging—which comes from a looser and

---

15 *Social Capital on Facebook: Differentiating Uses and Users* (May 2011)

more diverse set of relationships—typically enables access to new communication and opportunities such as job openings, because very close ties are likely to have redundant information.

The researchers classified activities on social networks into three categories. The first kind is directed communication with individual friends via chat or wall posts. The second involves passive consumption of social news by reading updates from others. Finally, there is broadcasting, which consists of updates not directed at any particular person.

The researchers concluded that directed communication has the potential to improve both bonding and bridging capital, due to the rich nature of the content and the strength of the relationship between the two communicators. In the case of one-on-one communication, both offering and receiving information increases the strength of relationships. Moreover, simply communicating one-on-one, due to the effort required relative to broadcast communication, signals the importance of a relationship.

For bridging social capital, only one-on-one communication increases social capital for senders on Facebook. Other forms of communication increase social capital only for the receiver. As the researchers point out, undirected broadcasts and passive consumption of news and updates may increase knowledge for the recipients and consumers of the news, but they don't further the development of relationships.

Broadcast communication is useful as a source of information about others that we can then use to increase the strength of relationships or to develop new friendships by referencing shared interests. In terms of casual acquaintances, putting out broadcasts doesn't buy us much, but receiving broadcasts and consuming news may. (Ironically, of course, recipients can only derive such value by nature of senders making the broadcasts.) The benefit of receiving broadcast information is greater for those with lower existing social communication skills.

The researchers also found that only a narrow set of major life changes have a significant impact on bridging social capital. Moving, for example, has a positive impact on bridging social capital, likely due to adding new relationships that diversify our access to information and resources. Losing one's job, however, has a negative impact, due to losing the social context associated with former co-workers.

Where does this leave us when it comes to the impact of changes in our personal relationships on our broader networks? Much as we worry about the impact of life changes such as marriage, divorce, death, family additions, new jobs, and illness on our broader social networks, in reality, while such events have a big impact on us personally, they have relatively little impact on our broader social networks.

How does this compare to increases and decreases in social capital via Facebook? Every time we double our one-to-one communication on the network, that results in about the same impact on bridging social capital as moving to a new city. It's equivalent to about half the impact associated with losing a job. In other words, a one-to-one digital message that establishes a new connection can have as much impact on bridging relationships as moving to a new city.

The implication is that, if we choose to take advantage of one-to-one communication online, social networks can greatly reduce the friction normally associated with expanding our broader networks. This may be one reason that when it comes to job searches, one-to-one messages on professional business networking site LinkedIn, even messages that come by way of a connection, are so effective.

While communication clearly plays a huge role in the development of relationships, information plays an important role as well. Although it may be somewhat less obvious, Google affects our relationships as well.

Ask nearly anyone who has been on an online date, and they will tell you that they've Googled their potential mate. According to It's Just Lunch, a dating service, 43 percent of singles have Googled their date before going out with them. And of the 1,167 singles surveyed, 88 percent said they wouldn't be offended if their date Googled them.[16]

Type virtually anyone's name into the search engine, and you'll see a series of results related to that person. They range from websites providing background information to articles someone has been mentioned in or written, to work profiles on LinkedIn.

The relative newness of Facebook, Twitter, and other forms of digital social communication means that academic research on the impact of such media is relatively limited. What is clear, however, is that one's online identity is a massive coalescence of Big Data.

When it comes to humans, Big Data is the information we share about ourselves in the form of photos, videos, status updates, tweets, and posts, and about our relationships, not to mention the digital trail we leave behind in the form of website clicks and online purchases.

Big Data And Romance: What The Future Holds

Enhancements to digital social communication, such as virtual gifts, may seem an unlikely way for people to communicate romantic

---

16 http://www.itsjustlunch.com

interest, but such forms of expression are becoming more and more commonplace. Virtual items like flowers that look like actual real world goods but only exist in digital form have become quite popular both in social games and on social networks. People have shown a willingness to pay for such digital goods.

One can imagine a future in which recommendation engines accurately predict what gifts will be most positively received and make suggestions to the senders. Of course, social networks might want to start by ensuring that partners simply don't forget each others' anniversaries.

Whether we want such insight or not, Big Data is both collecting and providing more information about us and our relationships. Algorithms such as those developed by Match.com to try to recommend better matches may be missing important data about how relationships evolve over time, but one can foresee a time when services integrated with Facebook or other platforms can provide better recommendations and predictions.

Indeed, Facebook may have more insight into our relationships over time than just about any other website. Blog site *All Facebook* cites a passage from *The Facebook Effect: The Inside Story of the Company That Is Connecting the World*, saying, "By examining friend relationships and communications patterns, [Zuckerberg, Facebook's co-founder and CEO] could determine with about 33 percent accuracy who a user was going to be in a relationship with..." a week in advance. Zuckerberg was apparently able to use data about who was newly single, who was looking at which profiles, and who was friends with whom to glean such insights.[17]

---

17 http://allfacebook.com/facebook-knows-that-your-relationship-will-end-in-a-week_b14374

Online dating and social communication are becoming more and more socially acceptable and are producing vast amounts of data in the process. Mass forms of communication are no substitute for one-to-one communication. But social networks that make such communication easier have the ability to reduce the amount of effort required to create new relationships and maintain existing ones dramatically. For now, algorithms such as those Match.com has developed may simply be a way to get those lower-friction forms of communication started.

As more people use smartphones like iPhone and Android devices, we're seeing mobile applications spring up for dating and as a more general way to meet new people. Applications such as Skout help users discover new friends wherever they are, whether at a local bar, at a sporting event, or while touring a new city. The application provides integrated ways to chat, exchange photos, and send gifts. Mobile applications will continue to reduce communication barriers and help us stay in touch with people we care about, all the while generating immense amounts of data that can help further refine interactions and introduce new connections.

Big Data may not yet be able to help an ailing relationship, but it can give us insight into the context surrounding our relationships, such as when the most difficult times of year are for relationships, based on the number of breakups that happen at those times.

Big Data may also help us figure out if a friend or relative is headed for trouble, by determining if he or she is communicating less frequently than normal, has an increased level of stress, or has experienced multiple major life events such as divorce, job loss, or the death of a relative or close friend that could lead to depression or other issues. At the same time, by continuing to make communication easier, Big Data may strengthen existing relationships and support the creation of new ones.

Ironic as it may seem, it is our desire to create new bonds and strengthen existing ones—our inherently social nature as human beings—that is one of the biggest drivers of the creation of technologies to help us communicate more easily.

We may not think of websites like Facebook or Google as Big Data Applications, because they are wrapped in easy-to-use, consumer-friendly interfaces. In fact, they epitomize Big Data.

It is easy in all the discussion of the size and economics of Big Data, of the talk of data streams and the lower costs of storing and analyzing data, to lose sight of the impact that Big Data has on our daily lives, whether we're talking about online matchmaking or predicting marital success. Not only can data open up new avenues for you to find the love of your life, in the future it may also help you hold onto that love once you find it.

Chapter Nine

How Big Data Is Changing The Way We Learn

Netflix can predict what movie you should watch next, and Amazon can tell what book you'll want to buy. With Big Data learning analytics, new online education platforms can predict which learning modules students will respond better to and help get students back on track before they drop out.[1] That's important given that the United States has the highest college dropout rate of any OECD country, with just 46 percent of college entrants completing their degree programs.[2] In 2009, the United States ranked fourteenth in reading, seventeenth in science, and twenty-fifth in math in a study of thirty-four OECD countries.[3]

Many students cite the high cost of education as the reason they drop out. At private, for-profit schools, 78 percent of attendees fail to graduate after six years, compared to a dropout rate of 45 percent for students in public colleges, according to a study by the Pew Research Center.[4]

---

1 http://www.ed.gov/edblogs/technology/files/2012/03/edm-la-brief.pdf

2 Organization for Economic Co-operation and Development, an organization whose mission is to promote policies that will improve economic and social well-being, and which counts thirty-four countries among its members.

3 http://www.msnbc.msn.com/id/40544897/ns/us_news-life/t/wake-up-call-us-students-trail-global-leaders/#.UNjIZ6WTVjY

4 http://www.pewsocialtrends.org/2011/05/15/is-college-worth-it/

Among eighteen- to thirty-four-year-olds without a college degree, 48 percent of those surveyed said they simply couldn't afford to go to college. Yet 86 percent of college graduates say that college was a good investment for them personally.

The data tells us that staying in school matters. But it also tells us that finishing school is hard to do. Paul Bambrick-Santoyo, Managing Director of Uncommon Schools Newark and author of *Driven By Data: A Practical Guide To Improve Instruction*, has shown that taking a data-driven approach makes a difference.

During the eight years in which Bambrick-Santoyo has been involved with the Uncommon Schools—a group of seven charter schools focused on helping students prepare for and graduate from college—the schools have seen significant gains in student achievement, reaching 90 percent proficiency levels on state assessments in many categories and grade levels.[5]

Using a data-driven approach can help us teach more effectively. At the same time, technology that leverages data can help students with day-to-day learning and staying in school.

Adaptive Learning Systems

How can computers help students learn more effectively? Online learning systems can evaluate past student behavior, both for individual students and across groups, and use that data to predict future student behavior. Within a given course or courseware framework, an adaptive learning system can decide what material to show a student next or determine which areas a student might not yet fully understand. It can also show students, visually, how

---

5 http://uncommonschools.org/bio/1017/paul-bambrick-santoyo

they are progressing with certain material, and how much material they've absorbed.

One of the strengths of an adaptive learning system is the built-in feedback loop it contains. Based on student interactions and performance, an adaptive learning system provides feedback to students, feedback to teachers, and feedback to the system itself, which humans or the system itself can then use to optimize the prediction algorithms used to help the students in the future. As a result, students, teachers, and systems have a lot more insight into what's going on.

Software can also predict which students are likely to need help in a given course.[6] Online courseware can evaluate factors such as log-in frequency and timeliness of turning in homework to predict whether students will pass or fail. Such software can then alert course instructors, who can reach out to students in danger of failing and offer them extra help or encouragement.

Knewton is one of the most well-known adaptive learning systems. Founded by a former executive of test prep company Kaplan, Knewton's system identifies the strengths and weaknesses of individual students. The company started out by offering GMAT test prep, but now universities are using it to improve education.

Arizona State University (ASU), the country's largest public university with some 72,000 students, uses the Knewton system to improve students' proficiency with math. After using the system for two semesters with two thousand students, ASU saw withdrawal rates drop by 56 percent and pass rates improve from 64 percent to 75 percent. The company has raised $54 million in venture capital,

---

6 http://www.nytimes.com/2012/07/22/education/edlife/colleges-awakening-to-the-opportunities-of-data-mining.html?_r=3&

and the World Economic Forum named Knewton a Technology Pioneer.

Dreambox, another provider of adaptive learning systems, is trying to improve math performance at the elementary school level. The company offers some 720 lessons that help boost math proficiency.

At a broader level, data mining can also recommend courses to students and determine whether college students are off-track in their selected major. ASU uses an eAdvisor system to coach students through college. The university's retention rate has risen from seventy-seven to 84 percent, a change that the provost, Elizabeth Capaldi, attributes to the eAdvisor system.[7]

The eAdvisor system tracks whether students fail key courses or don't sign up for them to begin with. It then flags such students so that academic advisors know to talk with them about their progress and recommend new majors, if necessary.

Such systems have vast amounts of data available to them, from individual course performance to standardized test scores to high school grades. To make appropriate course suggestions, they can compare data about any given student to data gathered about thousands of other students.

This increased level of transparency extends all the way from students to teachers to administrators. Students get more information about their own progress. Teachers get more visibility into individual student progress as well as overall class progress, and administrators can look across all classes at a school to see what's

---

7   https://asunews.asu.edu/20111012_eAdvisor_expansion and http://www.nytimes.com/2012/07/22/education/edlife/colleges-awakening-to-the-opportunities-of-data-mining.html

working and what isn't. District administrators can then draw conclusions about what kinds of educational programs, software, and approaches are most useful and adjust curriculums accordingly.

Putting Education Online

One of the most interesting uses of Big Data as applied to education is the ability of adaptive learning systems to test out many different educational approaches across a large number of students. Websites use A/B testing to show one version of a web page to one visitor and another version to another visitor. Learning systems can do the same thing.

A learning system can evaluate whether students learn faster when they receive a lot of practice on a given type of problem all at once, or when that practice is spread out over time. Learning systems can also determine how much material students retain after a given period of time and tie that back to the learning approaches used.

Big Data and education doesn't stop at understanding how students learn. New startups are bringing educational materials online, and in so doing, opening them up to a much larger audience.

Khan Academy is an online destination containing thousands of educational videos. Salman Khan, the founder of the site, originally started recording the videos himself, and the site now has more than 3,600 lectures available on a variety of topics including history, medicine, finance, biology, computer science, and more.[8] The site's videos are stored on YouTube, and in aggregate have received more than 202 million views.

---

8 http://en.wikipedia.org/wiki/Khan_Academy

The site's approach is simple, yet effective. In addition to thousands of short videos, which highlight the material being taught rather than the person teaching it, the site uses hundreds of exercises to help teach concepts and evaluate the level of each student's comprehension.

Codecademy, a startup, is focused on teaching people how to write software programs. Unlike Khan Academy, which relies heavily on videos, Codecademy focuses on interactive exercises. The site provides a series of courses grouped together in the form of tracks, such as the JavaScript track, the Web Fundamentals track, and the Ruby track, which enable users of the site to learn different programming languages.

It's a long way from there to being able to build and sell your own iPhone app—but the site provides a great place to get started. One can imagine courses from either site to train data scientists or educate business users on how to use analytics software.

Major universities are also putting their courses online. Harvard University and MIT teamed up to form edX, a not-for-profit enterprise that features learning designed specifically for study over the web. The site's motto is "The Future of Online Education: for anyone, anywhere, anytime." Six major universities now participate in the program. Along with MIT and Harvard, the University of California at Berkeley, The University of Texas, Wellesley, and Georgetown University are also participants.

University faculty members teach the classes, which typically consist of short lecture videos accompanied by assignments, quizzes, and exams. In addition to enabling these universities to deliver course material electronically, edX provides a platform for learning about how students learn. By analyzing student behavior, edX can determine which courses are most popular and which result in the greatest learning. The *MIT Technology Review* called offerings like edX the most important educational technology in the last two hundred years.[9]

Changing The Economics Of Education

As the *MIT Technology Review* points out, online learning isn't new. Some 700,000 students in the United States already use distance-learning programs. What's different is the scale at which new offerings operate, the technology used to deliver those offerings, and the low-cost or free delivery model.

As in other areas of Big Data, what's changed is not that Big Data never existed before, but the scale and cost at which it can be accessed. The power of Big Data is its ability not just to gather and analyze more data, but also to open up access to that data to a much larger number of people, and at a much lower cost. Free and low-cost educational offerings such as those from edX are called massive open online courses, or MOOCs for short.

In 2002, about 9.6 percent of college students were enrolled in at least one online course. By 2010, 31.3 percent of students were, according to a study by Babson Survey Research Group.[10] That means some 6.1 million college students are taking at least one course online every year.

Another offering, Coursera, was started by computer science professors at Stanford University. The company originally launched with Stanford, Princeton, the University of Michigan, and the

---

9 http://www.technologyreview.com/news/506351/the-most-important-education-technology-in-200-years/

10 http://sloanconsortium.org/publications/survey/going_distance_2011

University of Pennsylvania, and has since partnered with twelve more universities. It has received some 1.5 million course enrollments and has about 680,000 registered students.[11]

Meanwhile, uDemy, which has the tagline "the academy of you," brings together online instruction from a range of CEOs, best-selling authors, and Ivy League professors. The site takes a somewhat less academic approach to its offering and many of its courses are about practical business issues, such as raising venture capital. Unlike some of the other sites, uDemy allows course creators to provide their courses for free or charge for them.

uDacity, founded by Google vice president and part-time Stanford University professor Sebastian Thrun, has the goal of democratizing education. The company's initial courses have focused primarily on computer science related topics, but it is continuing to expand its offerings.

As existing academic institutions search for ways to remain relevant in an online world, it is clear that the proliferation of such digital offerings will offer insight into the most effective ways to deliver educational content. While you may not yet be able to get a degree from Harvard, MIT, or Stanford over the web, getting access to their materials, as well as to materials from anyone with something to teach, is becoming a lot easier.

Of course, online courses can't provide the same kind of social or physical experience that classrooms or laboratories can provide. Courses in biology, chemistry, and medicine require hands-on environments. And just as social encouragement and validation is important when it comes to exercising and dieting, it may also be

11 http://thenextweb.com/insider/2012/07/17/education-startup-coursera-partners-with-12-new-universities-raises-3-7m-and-hits-1-5m-students/

important when it comes to learning. The most promising educational systems of the future may be those that combine the best of the online and offline worlds.

Virtual environments may also provide a way to bring offline experiences online. The Virtual Medical Environments Laboratory adapts leading edge technology to provide medical training through simulation. Such simulation environments don't just take advantage of software but of hardware that simulates actual medical procedures. Such environments can also simulate the noise or distractions that medical personnel may experience in the real world.

Tracking Performance

The US government, across federal, state, and local governments, spends about $820 billion per year on education. That doesn't count all of the investment made at private institutions. But it does mean that administrators want visibility into how school systems are performing, and new systems are providing that visibility, according to Darrel M. West of the Brookings Institution.[12]

Dreambox, the adaptive learning systems provider, also provides visibility to administrators. In addition to delivering adaptive learning tools, it has a dashboard capability that aggregates data for administrators to view. Administrators can track student progress and see the percentage of students who have achieved proficiency.

At a government level, the United States Department of Education has created a dashboard that summarizes public school

---

12 http://www.brookings.edu/~/media/research/files/papers/2012/9/04%20
  education%20technology%20west/04%20education%20technology%20west

performance for the entire country. The interactive dashboard is available on the web at dashboard.ed.gov/dashboard.aspx.

States use a variety of different systems to report on educational progress. The state of Michigan provides a dashboard at www.michigan.gov/midashboard that indicates whether performance is improving, declining, or staying the same in areas such as third-grade reading proficiency, college readiness, and academic proficiency between grades three and eight.

The state's third-grade reading proficiency, for example, improved from 63.1 percent of students during the 2007–2008 school year, to 67.7 percent of students during the 2011–2012 school year. According to the site, this measure is a strong indicator of future academic success.

Such systems improve accountability and provide more visibility into educational performance, according to West. Much of the information that goes into such dashboards already exists, but web-based systems that have simple user interfaces and easy-to-view graphics are a big step forward in making such data more accessible and actionable.

Data mining, data analytics, adaptive learning solutions, and web dashboards all present opportunities to improve education and increase access to it. But one of the biggest challenges, states West, is the focus on "education inputs, not outputs." Quite frequently, schools are measured on seat-time, faculty-student ratios, library size, and dollars spent, rather than on results. "Educational institutions should be judged not just on what resources are available, but whether they do a good job delivering an effective education," says West.

When it comes to Big Data, education faces some of the same challenges as other areas. Incompatible technology systems make it hard for schools to aggregate data within schools, let alone compare data across different academic institutions. For example, some schools use separate systems for tracking academic performance and attendance.

How We Learn

As we talked about in the first chapter, data not only makes computers smarter—it also makes human beings smarter. But the biggest question of all when it comes to education and Big Data may be a fundamental question about education itself: how do we learn?

Different people learn in different ways. Some students do better with visual learning, while others do better with hands-on studies, or when they write things down. Psychologists spent much of the last century constructing theories about how people learn, but they made little progress in understanding how we learn.

About ten years ago, scientists started taking a different approach. They used neuroscience and cognitive psychology to study how the brain learns, rather than constructing theories.[13] What they discovered was that our ability to learn is shaped in large part not by what is taught but by the effectiveness of our learning process. A more efficient learning process can result in more effective learning.

According to one scientist, the popular notion that we only use 5 to 10 percent of our brains is wrong. In reality, we use the entire capacity of our brains.[14]

---

13 http://ideas.time.com/2011/10/12/the-science-of-how-we-learn/
14 http://clive-shepherd.blogspot.com/2007/02/science-of-learning.html

One of the keys to understanding how we learn is to recognize that our brains have limited resources for processing the huge amount of data we receive through all of our different senses. Our brains rely on all kinds of shortcuts to avoid getting swamped—what is known as cognitive overload.

As a result, to make learning more efficient, teachers can provide less information or take a very careful approach to how they communicate information. People have an easier time absorbing information if there's less noise that goes with it—but less noise also means less context.

One of the shortcuts the brain uses is to group things together. Teachers can make learning more efficient by grouping material so that students don't have to. Another approach to reducing cognitive overload is to remove every word or picture that isn't necessary to a particular learning goal. Challenging the brain helps with learning; researchers found that students learn more when they try to read a book for the first time than when they try to read the same book again.

Of course, all that still doesn't answer exactly *how* we learn. To cope with the vast amount of information it receives, the brain does a lot of filtering. The brain has evolved over many years, and one of the first things it needed to do was deal with basic survival.

Our ancestors were a lot more likely to survive if they could remember dangerous situations—such as stalking the wrong prey—and avoid them in the future. Such situations were often associated with moments of high emotion. As a result, it is easier for us to remember information that's associated with high emotion, whether it is positive or negative.[15]

---

15 http://www.illumine.co.uk/blog/2011/05/how-the-brain-absorbs-information/

Past experiences also influence how we retain information. Scientists believe that our brains store information in a sort of filing cabinet-like approach. This is one of the reasons it's easier to add more information to an existing area we know—an existing base of learning—than to learn something new from scratch.

Mathematics And The Brain

According to educational consultant Dr. David Sousa, citing Dr. Keith Devlin at Stanford University, mathematics is the study of patterns.[16] Sousa argues that all too often math is taught as simply a series of numbers and symbols, without any discussion of how it applies to daily life. Since meaning is one of the criteria the brain uses to identify whether information should be stored long-term, that lack of meaning may be one of the reasons some students struggle with math.

Devlin highlights a number of cases where math applies to real life. Using probability to determine odds, calculating the amount of interest you pay when you buy a car, and applying exponential growth curves to understanding population changes are three such examples.

But math may have as much to do with the language we use to represent our numbers as with how we learn it. As Malcolm Gladwell talks about in *Outliers*, referencing Stanislas Dahaene's book *The Number Sense*, the English numbering system is highly irregular. Unlike English numbers, which use words like eleven, twelve, and thirteen, Chinese, Korean, and Japanese numbers use a more logical and consistent approach: ten-one for eleven, ten-two for twelve, and the like.

16 http://howthebrainlearns.wordpress.com/author/clarkbarnett/

As a result, Asian children learn to count a lot faster. By four, Chinese children can count up to forty while American children of the same age can only count up to fifteen. They only learn to count to forty when they're a year older, putting them a year behind their Chinese counterparts. Gladwell cites another example: fractions. In Chinese three-fifths is literally, "out of five parts, take three," which makes such quantities much easier to work with: the language matches the concept.

The implications don't stop there. The brain has a working memory loop that can store about two seconds of information at a time. Chinese numbers can, in general, be pronounced in a shorter span of time than their English counterparts, which means that Chinese people can remember more numbers at a time.[17]

More math education is highly correlated with higher earnings. In a study by the Public Policy Institute of California, authors Heather Rose and Julian R. Betts found that students who had completed calculus courses had higher earnings than those who had only completed advanced algebra.[18] In turn, those students had higher earnings than people who had only completed basic algebra.

Higher-level math education is also associated with higher college graduation rates. As the authors point out, correlation is not the same as causation, but they conclude that math education is highly associated with both earnings and college graduation rates.

If there's one person who knows more about learning math than just about anyone else, it's Arthur Benjamin, Professor of Mathematics at Harvey Mudd College. Benjamin is best known for

---

17 http://www.gladwell.com/outliers/outliers_excerpt3.html
18 http://www.ppic.org/content/pubs/report/R_701JBR.pdf

his ability to perform *mathemagics*, in which he correctly multiplies large numbers in his head.

As Benjamin shows, math doesn't need to be boring. It can be fun and entertaining. Proving the point, his TED talk on mathemagics has received more than four million views. Benjamin has also authored a book: *Secrets of Mental Math: The Mathemagician's Guide to Lighting Calculation and Amazing Math Tricks*, as well as a DVD entitled *The Joy of Mathematics.* In his book, Benjamin shares a number of shortcuts to doing complex math in your head.

Language

So what about language? According to research by Dr. Patricia K. Kuhl at the Center for Mind, Brain, and Learning at the University of Washington, as infants, we store a lot of information about speech and language before we begin speaking. Simply listening to sounds tunes our brains to understand one language better than another.

Earlier we talked about how the brain filters the vast amount of information it is exposed to. The infant brain does much the same thing with language. As infants master the language spoken by their caretakers, they ignore sound differences that aren't relevant.

For example, the different sounds for 'r' and 'l' are important in English (for words like 'rake' and 'lake') but they aren't important in Japanese. Japanese babies tested at the age of six months could tell the difference between the two sounds equally as well as their American counterparts. By the age of ten to twelve months, however, infants in the US improved in their ability to tell the difference between the two sounds, while their Japanese counterparts got worse.

Kuhl attributes such changes to the infant brain focusing on the sounds it hears—the sounds of the infant's native language. During this period of rapid learning, it is also possible to reverse such declines by exposing infants to multiple languages. In one study, Kuhl had Chinese graduates students talk in Chinese with American infants. After twelve laboratory sessions, the American infants were able to recognize Chinese sounds just about as well as their Taiwanese counterparts. Kuhl concluded that the brains of infants encode and remember the patterns they hear well before speaking or even understanding complete words.

By the age of six months, our infant brains are able to map the patterns of language having to do with vowels and consonants and by nine months, patterns of words.[19] Kuhl describes the infant brain as analogous to a computer without a printer hooked up to it.

When it comes to reading, Kuhl's studies show that our ability to distinguish speech sounds at the age of six months correlates highly with language abilities like reading later in life. In other words, the better we are at distinguishing the basic building blocks of speech early in life, the better we are at complex language skills later in life.

According to Kuhl, we have about a trillion neurons (nerve cells) in place in our brains when we're born, but there are relatively few synaptic connections between. From the time we're born until about three years old, our brains form connections at a furious rate.

By age three, the brain of the average child has nearly twice as many connections as that of an adult. Moreover, the connections create three times more brain activity than in adults. At this point, the brain begins to prune unnecessary connections. Kuhl describes

---

19 http://www2.ed.gov/teachers/how/early/earlylearnsummit02/kuhl.pdf

this as "quite literally like a rose bush, pruning some connections helps strengthen others." The pruning process continues until the end of puberty.

Are you out of luck if you don't start learning multiple languages at a young age? Common wisdom has it that learning a new language is difficult, if not impossible, after childhood. But one adventurous individual spent more than nine years traveling the world to see how many new languages he could learn.

Much as mathematician Arthur Benjamin developed a set of shortcuts for doing rapid math calculations, Benny Lewis, author of the blog *Fluent in 3 Months: Unconventional Language Hacking Tips From Benny The Irish Polyglot* developed a set of shortcuts for rapidly learning to speak new languages. Lewis, a former electrical engineering student with a self-proclaimed dislike of learning new languages, has shown that learning a new language as an adult is possible, if you take the right approach.

According to Maneesh Sethi, author of *Hack The System*, most of the challenge in learning a language later in life is that we go about learning it the wrong way. Sethi realized after studying Spanish for four years in high school that he was an expert in Spanish, according to standardized tests. But, as he puts it, "I couldn't even order a burrito."[20]

Sethi breaks the strategy of rapid language learning down into four steps: having the right resources, which include a grammar book, memorization software, and films or books; getting a private tutor; speaking and thinking only in the new language; and finding friends and language partners to converse with.

---

20 http://lifehacker.com/5923910/how-i-learned-a-language-in-90-days

Sethi points out that by memorizing thirty words a day, you can learn 80 percent of the words necessary to communicate in a language. In Russian, for example, the seventy-five most common words make up 40 percent of occurrences. The 2,925 most common words make up 80 percent of occurrences—only seventy words fewer than the number you'll know by learning thirty new words per day. Sethi also highlights the importance of having the right mentality. Instead of thinking of himself as a blogger who wanted to learn Italian, he started thinking of himself as an "Italian learner (who blogs in his extra time)."

Fortunately, modern technology helps in many of the key areas, from memorization to tutoring to finding language partners. On the Mac, the Genius app uses a spaced repetition approach to flashcards that chooses questions intelligently based on your past performance. The more often you make a mistake, the more often the app will test you on a given word. The online site eduFire provides live, interactive tutoring sessions over the web.

Dealing With Data Overload

As children, we learn language by hearing it and speaking it, not by studying textbooks in a classroom. It should be no surprise therefore that the same approach that Kuhl highlights as being critical for children also works for adults: intensive, regular listening to and speaking the language we want to learn.

As Sethi points out, to learn a new language you must be "an active learner. Most people allow themselves to be taught to, but you have to take an active role in asking questions."

To cope with the vast amount of information it receives, the brain uses pattern matching and other shortcuts to make decisions.

In this context, the approaches taken by Lewis, Benjamin, and Sethi make perfect sense. Rather than waiting for the brain to develop new pattern matching approaches and turn those into shortcuts—which is hard work—the key is to teach the brain new shortcuts instead.

"The challenge isn't in learning a new language, but rather learning how to learn a language," says Sethi. The same may hold true for other areas of learning as well.

Ultimately, learning is about taking in information, storing it, and then making connections between what is already known and the newly acquired information.[21] When it comes to Big Data, one takeaway from research on the brain and how we absorb information is that more data may give us more insight, but ultimately, to be useful, it needs to be digested and filtered down to a set of actionable insights, insights that can have a direct impact on our decisions.

As applied to education, Big Data is already helping keep more students in school by figuring out when they're going to drop out. Adaptive learning solutions, whether in the form of complete systems or digital flashcard apps like Genius, are helping us learn more efficiently.

It's an exciting time for Big Data and education. Big Data holds the possibility of helping us become not just better teachers, but better students as well.

---

21 http://www.stanford.edu/class/ed269/hplintrochapter.pdf

Chapter Ten

Reaching More Customers With Better Data

The Big Data Conversation

No book on Big Data would be complete without a few words on the Big Data conversation. One of the biggest challenges to widespread adoption of Big Data is the nature of the Big Data conversation itself.

Historically, the discussion around Big Data has been a highly technical one. If the discussion remains that way, the benefits of Big Data will remain restricted to those with deep technical expertise. Good technology is critical. But companies must focus on communicating the business value they deliver in order for customers to buy their products, and for business leaders to embrace a culture of being data-driven.

In developing the Big Data Landscape, I talked with and evaluated more than a hundred vendors, from seed-stage startups to Fortune 500 companies. I spoke with numerous Big Data customers as well.

Many Big Data vendors lead with the technical advantages of their products to the exclusion of talking about business value, or vice versa. A technology-heavy company will often highlight the amount of information its database can store, or how many transactions its software can handle per second.

A vision-heavy company, meanwhile, will talk about how it plays in the Big Data space but will lack the concrete technical data to show why its solutions perform better, or the specifics about what use cases its product supports, and the problems it solves.

Effective communication about Big Data requires both vision and execution. Vision means telling the story and getting people excited about the possibilities. Execution means delivering on specific business-value, and having the proof to back it up.

Big Data cannot solve—at least not yet—a lack of clarity about what a product does, who should buy it, or the value a product delivers. Companies that lack clarity on these fronts struggle to sell their products, no matter how hard they try.

Thus, there are three key components in Big Data marketing: vision, value, and execution. "Earth's biggest bookstore," "The ultimate driving machine," and "A developer's best friend" all communicate vision clearly.

But clarity of vision alone is not sufficient. It must go hand in hand with clear articulation of the value a product provides, what it does, and who, specifically, should buy it.

Based on vision and business value, companies can develop individual stories that will appeal to the customers they're trying so hard to reach as well as to reporters, bloggers, and other members of industry. They can create effective blog posts, infographics, webinars, case studies, feature comparisons, and all the other marketing materials that go into successful campaigns—both to get the word out, and to support sales teams in selling your product.

Content, like other forms of marketing, needs to be highly targeted. The same person who cares about teraflops and gigabits won't care as much about which eight companies in the Fortune 500 use your solution. Both pieces of information are important—they simply matter to different audiences.

Even then, companies can generate a lot of awareness about their products but fail to convert prospects when they land on their websites. All too often, companies work incredibly hard to get visitors to their sites, only to stumble when it comes to converting those prospects into customers.

Website designers place buttons in non-optimal locations, give prospects too many choices of possible actions to take, or build sites that lack the information that customers want. It's all too easy to put a lot of friction in between a company and a customer who wants to download or buy.

When it comes to Big Data marketing, it's much less about traditional marketing and much more about creating an accessible conversation. By opening up the Big Data conversation, we can bring the benefits of Big Data to a much broader group of individuals.

Better Marketing With Big Data

Big Data itself can help improve the conversation. Marketers have analytics data from visitors to their websites, customer data from trouble ticketing systems, and actual product usage data— data that can help them close the loop in understanding how their marketing investments translate into customer behavior.

In 2011, marketers in the US spent $171.7 billion on advertising.[1] As spending on offline channels such as magazines, newspapers, and the yellow pages continues to decline, new ways to reach customers online keep springing up. Marketers spent $31.7 billion on online advertising in 2011, and are expected to invest more than $7 billion in mobile advertising in 2013.

Google remains the gorilla of online advertising, accounting for some 41.3 percent of total digital advertising revenue.[2] Meanwhile, social media such as Facebook, Twitter, and LinkedIn represent not only new marketing channels but new sources of data as well. From a Big Data perspective, the opportunity doesn't stop there.

Marketing today doesn't just mean spending money on ads. It means that every company has to think and act like a media company. It means not just running advertising campaigns and optimizing search engine listings, but developing content, distributing it, and measuring the results. Big Data Applications can pull the data from all these disparate channels together, analyze it, and make predictions about what to do next—either to help marketers make better decisions or to take action automatically.

Big Data And The CMO

By 2017, chief marketing officers (CMOs) will spend more on Information Technology than chief information officers (CIOs), according to industry research firm Gartner.[3] Marketing organi-

---

1 http://www.marketingcharts.com/television/politics-olympics-to-drive-almost-half-of-12-us-ad-revenue-growth-20894/

2 http://www.emarketer.com/newsroom/index.php/digital-ad-spending-top-37-billion-2012-market-consolidates/

3 http://www.zdnet.com/research-the-devalued-future-of-it-in-a-marketing-world-7000003989/

zations are making more of their own technology decisions, with less involvement from IT. More and more, marketers are turning to cloud-based offerings to serve their needs. That's because they can try out an offering and discard it if it doesn't perform.

Historically, marketing expenses have come in three forms: people to run marketing; the costs of creating, running, and measuring marketing campaigns; and the infrastructure required to deliver such campaigns and manage the results.

At companies that make physical products, marketers spend money to create brand awareness and encourage purchasing. Consumers purchase at retail stores, car dealerships, movie theaters, and other physical locations, or at online destinations such as Amazon.com.

Marketers at companies that sell technology products often try to drive potential customers directly to their websites. A technology startup, for example, might buy Google Adwords—the text ads that appear on Google's website and across Google's network of publishing partners—in the hopes that people will click on those ads and come to their website. From there, the potential customer might try out the company's offering or enter their contact information in order to download a whitepaper or watch a video, activities which may later result in the customer buying the company's product.

All of this activity leaves an immense digital trail of information, a trail that is multiplied ten times over, of course, because marketers don't just buy Google Adwords in order to drive customers to their websites. They buy many different kinds of ads across different ad networks and media types, and they can potentially collect data on the many different ways that customers interact with the company, from online chat sessions to phone calls to website visits to what product features a customer actually uses or even which segments of a particular video are most popular.

Historically, the systems required to create and manage marketing campaigns, track leads, bill customers, and provide helpdesk capabilities came in the form of expensive and difficult-to-implement installed enterprise software solutions. IT organizations would embark on the purchase of hardware, software, and consulting services to get the full suite of systems up and running to support marketing, billing, and customer service operations.

Cloud-based offerings have made it possible to run all of these activities via the Software as a Service (SaaS) model. Instead of having to buy hardware, install software, and then maintain such installations, companies can get the latest and greatest marketing, customer management, billing, and customer service solutions over the web.

Today, a significant amount of the data many companies have on their customers is now in the cloud, including corporate websites, site analytics, online advertising spend, trouble ticketing, and the like. A lot of the content related to company marketing efforts (such as press releases, news articles, webinars, slide shows, and other forms of content) are now online. Marketers at companies who deliver their products over the web, such as online collaboration tools or web-based payment systems, can now know which content a customer or prospect has viewed, along with demographic and industry information.

The challenge and opportunity for today's marketer is to put the data from all that activity together and make sense of it. For example, marketers might have their lists of customers stored in Salesforce.com, leads from their lead-generation activities stored in Marketo or Eloqua, and analytics that tell them about company website activity in Adobe Omniture or Google Analytics, a website analytics product from Google.

Certainly a marketer could try to pull all that data into a spreadsheet and attempt to run some analysis to determine what's working well and what isn't. But actually understanding the data takes significant analysis. Is a certain press release correlated with more website visits? Did a particular news article generate more leads? Do website visitors group into certain industry segments? What kind of content appeals to which kind of visitors? Did the movement of a button on a website result in more conversions once customers got to the company's website?

These are all questions that consumer packaged goods (CPG) marketers like Procter & Gamble (P&G) have focused on for years. In 2007, P&G spent $2.62 billion on advertising, and in 2010, the company spent $350 million on customer surveys and studies.[4] With the advent of Big Data, the answers are available not just to CPG companies who spend billions on advertising and hundreds of millions on market research each year, but also to big and small vendors alike across a range of industries. The promise of Big Data is that today's tech startup can have as much information about its customers and prospects as a big CPG company like P&G.

Another issue for marketers is understanding the value of customers, and in particular how profitable they are. For example, a customer who spends a small amount of money but has lots of support requests is probably unprofitable. Yet it is very hard to correlate trouble-ticket data with product-usage data, and information about how much revenue a particular customer generated, with how much it cost to acquire that customer.

---

4 http://www.valueline.com/Stocks/Highlight.aspx?id=9552 and http://www.chacha.com/question/how-much-does-p%26g-spend-on-advertising

Big Data Marketing In Action

Although few companies are able to analyze such vast amounts of data in a cohesive manner today, one thought leader who has been able to perform such analysis is Patrick Moran, vice president of marketing at New Relic. New Relic is an application performance monitoring company. The company makes tools that help developers figure out what's causing websites to run slowly, and make them faster.

Moran has been able to pull together data from systems like Salesforce.com and demand-generation system Marketo, along with data from Zendesk, a helpdesk ticketing system, and from Twitter campaigns, on which New Relic spends some $150,000 per month. In conjunction with a data scientist, Moran's team is able to analyze all that data and figure out which Twitter campaigns have the most impact—down to individual tweets. That helps Moran figure out which campaigns to spend more on in the future.

The first step in Moran's ability to gather and analyze all that data is having it in the cloud. Just as New Relic itself is a SaaS company, virtually all of the systems from which Moran's team gathers marketing data are cloud-based as well.

The next step in the process is running a series of marketing campaigns by investing in ads across Google, Twitter, and other online platforms.

Third, the marketing team gathers all the data from Salesforce. com, Marketo, Twitter campaigns, product-usage data, and other forms of data in one place. In New Relic's case, they store the data in Hadoop.

Fourth, using the open-source statistics package R, the team analyzes the data to determine the key factors that drive the most revenue. For example, they can evaluate the impact on revenue of the customer's geographic location, the number of helpdesk tickets a customer submitted, the path the customer took on New Relic's website, the tweets a customer saw, the number of contacts a customer has had with a sales rep, and the kind of performance data the customer monitors within the New Relic application. By analyzing all of this data, Moran's team even knows at what time of day to run future campaigns. Finally, the team runs a new set of campaigns based on what they've learned.

New Big Data Applications are emerging specifically to make the process that teams like Moran's follow easier. MixPanel, for example, is a web-based application that allows marketers to run segmentation analysis, understand their conversion funnels (from landing page to product purchase), and perform other kinds of marketing analysis.

The promise of Big Data is that by aggregating all of this information about customer activity, from ad campaign to trouble ticket to product purchase, it is possible for Big Data marketers to correlate all of these activities and not only reach more potential customers but to reach them more efficiently.

Marketing Meets The Machine

The next logical step in Big Data marketing is not just to bring disparate sources of data together to provide better dashboards and insights for marketers, but to use Big Data to automate marketing. This is tricky, however, because there are two distinct components of marketing: creative and delivery.

The creative component of marketing comes in the form of design and content creation. A computer, for example, can't design the now famous "For everything else, there's MasterCard" campaign. But it can determine whether showing users a red button or a green button, a twelve-point font or a fourteen-point font, results in more conversions. It can figure out, given a set of potential advertisements to run, which ones are most effective.

Given the right data, a computer can even optimize particular elements of a text or graphical ad for a particular person. For example, an ad-optimization system could personalize a travel ad to include the name of the viewer's city: "Find the lowest fares between San Francisco and New York" instead of just "Find the lowest fares."[5] It can then determine whether including such information increases conversion rates.

In theory, a human being could perform such customizations, and in the past, we have. Graphic artists used to—and some still do—customize each ad individually. Web developers would set up a few different versions of a web page and see which one did the best. The problem with such approaches is not only that they're very limited in terms of the number of different layouts, colors, and structures a marketer can try, but there's also no easy way to customize what is shown to people with different profiles. A different button location, for example, might work better for one group of potential customers, but not for another.

What's more, it's virtually impossible to perform such customizations for thousands, millions, or billions of people. And that is the scale at which online marketing operates. Google, for example, serves an average of nearly thirty billion ad impressions per day.[6] That's where Big Data systems excel: when there is a large volume

---

5 http://www.adopsinsider.com/ad-ops-basics/dynamic-creative-optimization-where-online-data-meets-advertising-creative/

6 http://www.business2community.com/online-marketing/how-many-ads-does-google-serve-in-a-day-0322253

of data to deal with, and when such data must be quickly processed and acted upon.

Some solutions are emerging that perform automated modeling of customer behavior to deliver personalized ads. Solutions like TellApart, a retargeting application, are putting together automated analysis of customer data with the ability to display relevant advertisements based on that data. TellApart identifies shoppers who have left a retailer's website and delivers personalized ads to them when they visit other websites, based on the interests that a given shopper showed while browsing the retailer's site. This kind of personalized advertising brings shoppers back to the retailer's site, often resulting in a purchase. By analyzing shopper behavior, TellApart is able to target high-quality customer prospects, while avoiding those who aren't ultimately likely to make a purchase.

When it comes to marketing, automated systems are primarily involved in large scale ad serving and in lead-scoring, that is, rating a potential customer lead based on a variety of pre-determined factors, such as the source of the lead. These activities lend themselves well to data-mining and automation, because they are well-defined processes with specific decisions that need to be made, such as determining whether a lead is good or not—and results that can be fully automated, such as choosing which ad to serve.

Plenty of data is available to help marketers—and marketing systems—optimize content creation and delivery. The challenge is putting it to work.

Social media scientist Dan Zarrella has studied millions of tweets, likes, and shares, and he has produced quantitative research on what words are associated with the most re-tweets, the optimal time of day to blog, and the relative importance of photos, text, video, and links.[7] The next step in Big Data meets the machine will be Big Data Applications that combine research like Zarrella's with automated content campaign management.

In the years ahead, we'll see intelligent systems continue to take on more and more aspects of marketing: not just scoring leads, but also determining which campaigns to run and when to run them, and displaying the ideal website for every visitor. Marketing software won't just be about dashboards that help humans make better decisions. With Big Data, marketing software will be able to run campaigns and optimize the results.

The Big Data Content Engine

When it comes to creating content for marketing, there are really two distinct kinds of content most companies need to create: high-volume and high-value. Amazon, for example, has some 248 million pages stored in Google's search index.[8] Such pages are known as the "long tail." People don't come across any individual page all that often, but when someone is searching for a particular item, it's there to be found. Consumers searching for products are highly likely to come across an Amazon page while performing their search.

Human beings can't create each of those pages. Instead, Amazon automatically generates its pages from its millions of product listings. The company creates pages that describe individual products as well as category pages that are amalgamations of multiple products: there's a headphones page, for example, that lists all the different kinds of headphones along with individual headphones and text

---

7   http://danzarrella.com
8   http://blog.hubspot.com/blog/tabid/6307/bid/21729/3-Marketing-Lessons-From-Amazon-s-Web-Strategy.aspx

about headphones in general. Each page, of course, can be tested and optimized.

Amazon has the advantage not only of having a huge inventory of products—its own and those listed by merchants that partner with Amazon—but a rich repository of user-generated content, in the form of product reviews, as well. Amazon combines a huge Big Data source, a product catalog, with a huge amount of user-generated content.

This makes Amazon not only a leading product seller, but also a leading source of great content. In addition to reviews, Amazon has product videos, photos (both Amazon and user-supplied), and other forms of content. Amazon reaps the rewards of this in two ways: it is likely to be found in search engine results, and users come to think of Amazon as having great content (not just great products) and start going there directly to do product research, making them more likely to make a purchase on the site.

Other companies, particularly e-commerce companies with existing large, online product catalogs, have turned to solutions like Bloomreach. Bloomreach works with websites to generate pages for the search terms that shoppers use. For example, while an e-tailer might identify a product as a kettle, a shopper might search for the term "hot pot." The Bloomreach solution ensures that sites display relevant results to shoppers, regardless of the exact search term the shopper uses.

Amazon isn't the only company that wouldn't traditionally be considered a media company that has turned itself into exactly that. Business networking site LinkedIn has too. In a very short time, *LinkedIn Today* has become a powerful new marketing channel. It has transformed the business social-networking site into an authoritative source of content and delivered a valuable service to the site's users in the process.

LinkedIn used to be a site that users would occasionally frequent when they wanted to connect with someone, or they were starting a new job search. *LinkedIn Today* made the site relevant on a daily basis by curating relevant news from around the web and updates from users of the site itself.

LinkedIn goes a step further than most traditional media sites by showing users content that is relevant to them based on their interests. The site brings users back via a daily e-mail that contains previews of the latest news. LinkedIn has created a Big Data content engine that drives new traffic, keeps existing users coming back, and maintains high levels of engagement on the site.

How can a company that doesn't have millions of users or product listings create content at Big Data scale? We'll answer that question in a moment—but first, a few words on marketing and buying Big Data products.

The New PR

When it comes to driving demand for products and keeping prospects engaged, it's all about content creation: blog posts, infographics, videos, podcasts, slide decks, webinars, case studies, e-mails, newsletters, and other materials are the fuel that keep the content engine running.

Since 1980, the number of journalists "has fallen drastically, while public relations people have multiplied at an even faster rate."[9] In 1980, there were .45 public-relations (PR) workers per 100,000 people, compared to .36 journalists. In 2008 there were twice as

---

9 http://www.propublica.org/article/pr-industry-fills-vacuum-left-by-shrinking-newsrooms/single

many PR workers, .90 for every 100,000 people, compared with .25 journalists. That means there are more than three PR people for every journalist, which makes getting your story covered by a reporter harder than ever before. That means that companies, Big Data and otherwise, have to create useful and relevant content themselves to compete at Big Data scale.

In many ways, content marketing is the new advertising. As of 2011, according to NM Incite, a Nielsen/McKinsey company, there were some 181 million blogs worldwide, compared to only thirty-six million in 2006.[10] But the good news for companies trying to get the word out about their products is that many of these blogs are consumer blogs, and creating a steady stream of high-quality content is difficult and time-consuming. A lot more people consume content than create it. A study by Yahoo research[11] showed that about twenty thousand Twitter users generated 50 percent of all tweets.[12]

Content marketing means putting as much effort into marketing your product as you put into marketing the content you create about your product. Building great content no longer means simply developing case studies or product brochures specifically about your product, but delivering news stories, educational materials, and entertainment.

In terms of education, IBM, for example, has an entire portfolio of online courses. Vacation rental site Airbnb created Airbnb TV to showcase Airbnb properties in cities around the world, which in the process showcased Airbnb itself. You can no longer just market

---

10 http://blog.nielsen.com/nielsenwire/online_mobile/buzz-in-the-blogosphere-millions-more-bloggers-and-blog-readers/

11 http://research.yahoo.com/pub/3386

12 http://blogs.hbr.org/cs/2012/12/if_youre_serious_about_ideas_g.html

your product; you have to market your content marketing too, and that content has to be compelling in its own right.

Crowdsource Your Way To Big Data Scale

Producing all that content might seem like a daunting and expensive task. It needn't be. Crowdsourcing, which involves distributing tasks to people, is an easy way to generate that form of unstructured data that is so critical for marketing: content.[13]

Many companies already use crowdsourcing to generate articles for search engine optimization (SEO), articles that help them get listed—and more highly ranked—in search engines. Many people associate such content crowdsourcing with high-volume, low-value forms of content. But today it is possible to crowdsource high-value, high-volume content as well.

Crowdsourcing does not replace in-house content development, but it can augment it. A wide variety of sites now provide crowdsourcing services. Amazon Mechanical Turk (AMT) is frequently used for tasks like content categorization and content filtering, which are difficult for computers, but easy for humans. Amazon itself uses AMT to determine if product descriptions match their images. Other companies connect to the programming interfaces that AMT supports to deliver vertical-specific services such as audio and video transcription.[14]

Sites like Freelancer.com and oDesk.com are frequently used to find software engineers, or to create large volumes of low-cost articles for SEO purposes, while sites like 99designs and Behance make

---

13 http://en.wikipedia.org/wiki/Crowdsourcing
14 Speechpad.com, in which the author is an investor, is one such example.

it possible for creative professionals, such as graphic designers, to showcase their work, and for content buyers to line up designers to deliver creative work. Meanwhile, companies like TaskRabbit are applying crowdsourcing to offline tasks such as food delivery, shopping, house cleaning, and pet sitting.

One of the primary differences between relatively low value content created exclusively for online marketing purposes and high value content is the authoritative nature of the latter. Low-value content tends to provide good fodder for the search engines in the form of an article written to catch a particular keyword search. High-value content, in contrast, tends to read or display more like professional news, education, or entertainment content. Blog posts, case studies, thought leadership pieces, technical write-ups, infographics, video interviews, and the like fall into this category. This kind of content is also the kind that people want to share. Moreover, if your audience knows that you have interesting and fresh content, that gives them more reason to come back to your site on a frequent basis, and a higher likelihood of staying engaged with you and your products.

The key to such content is that it must be newsworthy, educational, entertaining, or better yet, a combination of all three. The good news for companies struggling to deliver this kind of content is that crowdsourcing now makes it easier than ever.

Crowdsourcing can come in the form of using a website like 99designs, but it doesn't have to. As long as you provide a framework for content delivery, you can plug in crowdsourcing to generate the content. For example, if you create a blog for your website, you can author your own blog posts, but also publish those authored by contributors, such as customers and industry experts.

If you create a TV section of your site, you can post videos that are a mix of videos you create yourself, videos embedded from other sites such as YouTube, and videos produced through crowdsourc-ing. Those producers can be your own employees, contractors, or industry experts conducting their own interviews. You can crowd-source webinars and webcasts in much the same way. Simply look for people who have contributed content to other sites and contact them to see if they're interested in participating on your site.

Using crowdsourcing is an efficient way to keep your high-value content production machine humming. It simply requires a content curator or a content manager to manage the process.

Marketing Your Content

In addition to creating content that's useful in the context of your own website, it's also critical to create content others will want to share, and that bloggers and news outlets will want to write about. That means putting together complete content packages. Just as you would include an image or video along with a blog post on your own site, you should do the same when creating content you intend to pitch to others.

Some online writers are now measured and compensated based on the number of times their posts are viewed. As a result, the easier you make it for them to publish your content and the more com-pelling content you can offer them, the better. For example, a press release that comes with links to graphics that could potentially be used alongside an article is easier for a writer to publish than one that doesn't.

A post that is ready to go, in the form of a guest post, for ex-ample, is easier for an editor or producer to work with than a press release. An infographic that comes with some text describing what its key conclusions are is easier to digest than a graphic by itself.

Once your content is published, generating visibility for it is key. Simply announcing a product update is no longer sufficient. High-volume, high-quality content production requires a media company-like mindset. Crowdsourcing is still in its infancy, but we can expect the market for it to continue to grow in the coming years.

Measuring The Results

On the other end of the spectrum from content creation is analyzing all that unstructured content to understand it. Computers use natural language processing and machine learning algorithms to understand unstructured text, such as the half billion tweets that Twitter processes every day. This kind of Big Data analysis is referred to as sentiment analysis or opinion mining.

By evaluating posts on Internet forums, tweets, and other forms of text that people post online, computers can determine whether consumers view brands positively or negatively. Companies like Radian6, which Salesforce.com acquired for $326 million in 2010, and Collective Intellect, which Oracle acquired in 2012, perform this kind of analysis. Marketers can now measure overall performance of their brand and individual campaign performance as well.

Yet despite the rapid adoption of digital media for marketing purposes, measuring the return on investment (ROI) from marketing remains a surprisingly inexact science. According to a survey of 243 CMOs and other executives, 57 percent of marketers don't base their budgets on ROI measures.[15] Some 68 percent of respondents said they base their budgets on historical spending levels, 28 per-

---

15 http://adage.com/article/cmo-strategy/study-finds-marketers-practice-roi-preach/233243/

cent said they rely on gut instinct, and 7 percent said their marketing spending decisions weren't based on any metrics.

The most advanced marketers will put the power of Big Data to work—removing more unmeasurable components from their marketing efforts, and continuing to make their marketing efforts more data-driven, while others will continue to rely on traditional metrics such as brand awareness, or no measurement at all. This will mean a widening gap between the marketing haves, and the marketing have-nots.

While marketing at its core will remain creative, the best marketers will use tools to optimize every e-mail they send, every blog post they write, and every video they produce. Ultimately every part of marketing that can be done better by an algorithm—choosing the right subject line or time of day for example—will be. Just as so much trading on Wall Street is now done by quants, large portions of marketing will be automated in the same way.[16] Creative will pick the overall strategy, but quants will run the execution.

Of course, great marketing is no substitute for great product. Big Data can help you reach prospective customers more efficiently. It can help you better understand who your customers are, and how much they're spending. It can optimize your website so those prospects are more likely to convert into customers once you've got their attention. But in an era of millions of reviews, and news that spreads like wildfire, great marketing alone isn't enough. Delivering a great product is still job one.

---

16 http://www.b2bmarketinginsider.com/strategy/real-time-marketing-trading-room-floor

About The Author

David Feinleib is the producer of *The Big Data Landscape*, *Big Data Trends*, and *Big Data TV*, all of which may be found on the web at www.BigDataLandscape.com. Mr. Feinleib's *Big Data Trends* presentation was featured as "Hot On Twitter" and has been viewed more than 30,000 times on SlideShare.

Mr. Feinleib has been quoted by *Business Insider* and *CNET*, and his writing has appeared on *Forbes.com* and in *Harvard Business Review China*. He is the Managing Director of The Big Data Group.

Prior to The Big Data Group, Mr. Feinleib was a general partner at Mohr Davidow Ventures. Mr. Feinleib co-founded Consera Software, which was acquired by HP; Likewise Software, which was acquired by EMC Isilon; and Speechpad, a leader in web-based audio-video transcription. He began his career at Microsoft.

Mr. Feinleib holds a BA from Cornell University, graduating *summa cum laude*, and an MBA from the Graduate School of Business at Stanford University. He is an avid violinist and an Ironman finisher.

Made in the USA
San Bernardino, CA
10 February 2014